Angels & Goddesses

Celtic Christianity & Paganism in Ancient Britain

By Michael Howard

Angels & Goddesses
Celtic Christianity & Paganism in Ancient Britain

©1994 Michael Howard

ISBN 1 898307 03 2

First printed Jan 1994
Reprinted Oct 1994
Reprinted July 1995
Reprinted Dec 1995
Reprinted Sept 1996
Reprinted Dec 1997

Cover illustration by Simon Rouse

Published by:

Capall Bann Publishing
Freshfields
Chieveley
Berks
RG20 8TF

b

In Memory of

Christine Hartley

Acknowledgements

I would like to thank Carolyn Inglis, Dr Jill Venus, Catherine Johnson, Dave Clark, and their staff and Dr Maureen Lofmark of the Department of Continuing Education at St David's University College (University of Wales), Lampeter, West Wales for their teaching, help and support which made this book possible. I would also like to thank Professor George Wells for editing my research notes and providing information on St Alban, Keith Morgan and Anna Greenslade for taking me to St Beuno's church at Pistyll in North Wales, Peter Dickens for pointing me towards the role of St Columba as a seer , Mike Harris, Canon Curtis Hayward and Basil Wilby for providing information and contacts for the chapter on Celtic Christianity today and last, but not least, Judith Mayhew for her encouragement and inspiration.

M.H.

Contents

Introduction

If you believe some historical accounts and textbooks, Christianity arrived in Britain in 597 CE. This was when Pope Gregory sent Augustine to convert the heathen Anglo-Saxons. The popular version of how this happened relates that the Pope was wandering around the slave market in Rome when he saw some young boys for sale. They had fair complexions and when he asked the slave trader where they came from he was told "From the island of Britain", where the people still practised paganism and were known as Angles. The Pope responded that this was a fitting name because the boys looked like angels. It was then he decided to send a mission to convert these heathen islanders to Christianity.

This is a nice fairy tale, even if it seems a little strange that Gregory was more interested in the souls of the boy slaves then apparently freeing them from their material bondage. The impression given by this story, which I remember vividly from Sunday school as a child, is that Christianity did not arrive in these islands until the end of the 6th century, and when it did come it was the Roman Catholic version. In fact there is a wealth of evidence, both historical and legendary, suggesting Christianity arrived in Britain during the period of Roman occupation and was possibly established here shortly after the crucifixion. Certainly by the time of the belated arrival of Pope Gregory's mission led by Augustine the Christian faith was actively being practised in the British Isles in a uniquely Celtic form. Not only that, but its priests were heavily engaged in an epic struggle with the indigenous pagan Old Religion.

The purpose of this book is to trace the development of the early forms of Christianity from Roman times to the arrival of Augustine and its survival, in the guise of Celtic Christianity, into the Middle Ages. Indeed, as I hope to prove, the ideas and philosophy behind Celtic Christianity have survived into the present-day and, with the rise of the New Age movement, are undergoing something of a popular revival. As will be seen at the end of this book, these unique Celtic Christian beliefs may be relevant to modern issues and spiritual developments such as the threat to the environment, feminism, the neo-pagan revival and the radical changes affecting the Church today.

What initially interested me when I began to study this subject, as a research project on Celtic Christianity in Wales at St David's University, Lampeter in West Wales, was the way in which early Christianity in ancient Britain absorbed the native paganism.. In fact the early Church fought with and was heavily influenced by the earlier forms of spirituality the Christian missionaries encountered. This can be seen both in the history of early Christianity in Roman Britain and in the Celtic Church, where pagan and Christian beliefs co-existed, albeit in an uneasy and sometimes violent relationship.

In its attempt to eradicate paganism the Church took over many of the heathen festivals, transformed some of the Old Gods into saints and destroyed pagan temples to replace them with churches. It is often thought that this process began with Pope Gregory's famous letter to Augustine, instructing him to take over the pagan shrines for Christian worship, but, as I shall show, it was a program that began in the early days of Christianity in Roman Britain and was actively followed by the pre-Augustinian Celtic Church.

In order to place early and Celtic Christianity into its proper historical and spiritual context the book opens with a brief description of the Celts and their religious beliefs, including druidism. This section presumes that the reader will have some background knowledge of this subject or, at least, can follow up the material provided here with further reading. Chapter One also describes the struggle between early Christianity and the pagan mystery religions and ends with the arrival of the Romans in Britain and their destruction of the druidic sanctuary on Anglesey, North Wales. In the second chapter legendary accounts of the establishment of the British Church in Britain by disciples of Jesus are described. This chapter also describes the persecution of the early Christians including St Alban, by the Roman Emperors and it ends with the lives of Maximus, the last Roman Governor of Wales and his Welsh wife, Elen, who planted the seeds of Celtic Christianity in Britain.

Chapter Three begins with the arrival of the pagan Saxons in south-east England and the take-over of pagan sacred sites by the Celtic Christians. It also deals with the monastic tradition and the influence of the Middle Eastern desert hermits on Celtic Christianity. In Chapter Four, on the Age of the Saints in the 5th and 6th centuries CE, the Pelagian heresy is described and the life and work of St David, patron saint of Wales. Chapter Five shows how these Celtic holy men and women not only battled with pagan beliefs, but were influenced by the continuing practice of the Old Ways among the people they were trying to convert. In Chapter Six we look at the Irish Church and the lives of SS Patrick and Brigid. With Chapter Seven the arrival of Augustine is described and his struggle with the Celtic Church as they resisted domination from Rome. This chapter also deals with the revivals of paganism that threatened the existence of Christianity.

Chapter Eight is on the Northumbrian mission with information on the northern Celtic saints, the Synod of Whitby and the coming of the Vikings, while Chapter Nine deals with the survival of Celtic Christianity in the medieval Grail romances and the 18th century neo-druidic revival. Finally, the last chapter brings the story up to date with the revival of Celtic Christianity today and its possible relevance to green spirituality, feminism and modern neo-paganism.

Because of the nature of the subject matter, my primary sources have been the standard works on Roman Britain, the Celtic saints and the medieval history of the Church. I have attempted, where possible, to stay within the boundaries of historical fact (whatever that mythical beast is!) However, I have also interpreted this material freely and indulged in some speculation, as do all writers dealing with historical subjects.

Due to my personal background as a researcher and student of mythology, folklore and ancient religions, I have dealt with the subject matter from an esoteric viewpoint and perspective. No doubt there will be those who disapprove of this approach and will disagree with what I have to say in this context. This book represents my personal view of history of early Christianity and its relationship with the old pagan religions and anyone is at liberty to challenge it.

The general aim of the book is not to produce a dry, academic history of early Christianity, but to illustrate the transition between paganism and the new Christian religion and how each belief system was dramatically changed by contact with the other. A high percentage of the material in this book derives from Welsh sources and this is a non-deliberate bias created by the availability of these sources. Also, of course, Celtic Christianity flourished in its most virile form in Wales and influenced other regions of ancient Britain. However, hopefully, I have not neglected other areas of the British Isles and I have attempted to provide a broad and overall picture of the development and spread of the Celtic Church.

Michael Howard

West Wales

Samhain 1993

Chapter One
Celts, Druids & Christians

The origins of the Celts, as a separate people with a distinctive racial identity, are difficult to trace in the mists of prehistory which shroud our knowledge of ancient Europe. As the Celts were an oral, rather then a literary, based civilisation and left no written records of their passage through history, any attempt to identify their origins and describe their culture and religion has to be achieved through the less then accurate medium of archaeology and the accounts left by those races who conquered them.

The archaeologist identifies the Celts from the physical evidence they left, while those who study languages claim to be able to recognise the Celts from the traces of their unique language. Whichever method is used to identify the Celts as a separate racial grouping from the Megalithic and Bronze Age peoples of prehistoric Europe it is obvious that around 1000 BCE a distinct 'Celtic' culture emerged from these earlier societies in Central Europe. By the 3rd century BCE this Celtic culture was firmly established across the European continent from Iberia (Spain and Portugal) in the south, to the Ukraine in and southern Germany in the north, the British Isles in the west and northern Italy in the east.

Our interest is not in the materialistic aspects of Celtic society, interesting though they may be, but in the spiritual belief system and religious observances that were practised within it. In the past the standard historical textbooks have been less then kind to the inhabitants of ancient Britain. When I was a child in the 1950s the Celts were still being represented as woad-painted savages who were civilised by the Romans. Vaguely I also believed these 'Ancient Britons' had built Stonehenge, a fantasy which dates back to the 18th century antiquarians involved in the neo-druidic revivalist. This confusion between the Megalithic culture and the Celts is not likely to go away. Even the Welsh Tourist Board in its glossy brochures misrepresents Megalithic cromlechs and stone circles as examples of (Welsh) Celtic heritage.

Although the druids were not responsible for building Stonehenge they may have known its astronomical secrets and, like the earlier Megalithic people, used it as a solar-lunar temple. This is of course purely speculative and has not been confirmed by historical fact. Merlin, who was probably a druid or even a prehistoric shaman, is credited with magically transporting the Stonehenge from Ireland (West Wales?) This legend may, or may not, be a folk memory of the druidic use of the henge in Celtic times.

Certainly the archaeological finds and historical research of the last fifty years have dramatically changed our perception of the Celts and increased our knowledge of these ancient people. Few people nowadays can really believe British history began with the arrival of the Romans. Ironically, all this research has thrown up more questions then it has been able to answer and exposed how very little we actually know about the religious beliefs of our ancestors. For instance the Celts may not have built Stonehenge, but there is archaeological evidence for what some experts describe as 'proto-druidism' pre-existing their arrival on the historical scene.

In a popular form, this idea first surfaced in the public domain in an article in The Independent newspaper in June 1988. This article said some archaeologists were of the belief that druidism pre-dated the Celtic period as an organised religious system. They suggested there may have been a continuity of religious belief and practice dating back to at least 7000 BCE. This allegedly proto-druidic, pre-Celtic religious cultus involved a number of key elements including the worship of water deities, sacrificial offerings, the sacred symbolism of weapons, the use of circle and spiral motifs in religious art, the employment of astronomical, astrological and calenderical observation as part of a seasonal cycle of religious festivals, the sanctity of fire, the worship of trees and stones and the sacredness of the number three.

This alleged continuity of religious belief from Megalithic times could explain the association of Celtic gods and goddesses, and later the Celtic saints, with prehistoric sacred sites. It could also, of course, offer an explanation for the historical and folkloric association between druids and Megalithic sites. When the Roman missionaries arrived in Britain in the 6th century they found its pagan inhabitants using prehistoric standing stones, stone circles and burial mounds for religious purposes. If local folklore can be believed, these prehistoric sites were still being used by witches in the Middle Ages - and still are today.

This is very much a chicken-and-egg theory, for continuity of religious belief is obviously a factor in the development of any culture or in any cultural take-over or interchange. It is evident that the Celts did not appear in history from thin air but that the 'Celtic' culture developed from earlier models. It is also evident that the Celts adopted some of the religious elements of the Megalithic and Bronze Age peoples they conquered. The Indo-European religion of the Celtic races, which has features in common with both the Iranian and Hindu belief systems, would have also introduced new elements into the native paganism which existed before the Celts arrived in Western Europe. Indeed many of the religious elements described in. The Independent article survived Celtic paganism and can be found in the strange mixture of Christian and pagan beliefs which co-existed until the medieval period and beyond.

What seems doubtful is that druidism per se, representing the belief system of the priestly caste in Celtic society, existed as a separate and identifiable entity before the arrival of the Celts. It has been speculated that an elite of priests and/or priestesses must have existed in prehistoric Europe within the Megalithic and Bronze Age cultures. This elite, it has been suggested, were behind the impressive organisation and supervision of the construction work responsible for the burial mounds, stone circles and standing stones. Were they, however, 'druids' as we would understand the meaning of that term today?

This question must remain unanswered because of the lack of real knowledge we possess about the Megalithic period and the emergence of the Celts as a ethnic group throughout Europe. As an example of the confusion surrounding the subject, a few months after *The Independent* article was published, Professor Colin Frew of Cambridge University, writing in *The Listener* magazine (20th October 1988), suggested that the builders of Stonehenge may have spoken an Indo-European language. He further claimed that the popular image of Aryan 'warlike horsemen' riding out of the east, so beloved of modern feminist historians, was a 19th century fantasy. Instead of violent racial migrations changing prehistory, Frew's conceptual model imagines instead a gradual process of cultural innovations developing with fairly stable societies. This appears to support the idea of external sources shaping ancient societies but in fact Renfrew claims this is a fallacy. It is hoped the question can be finally resolved with the recent development of new techniques for isolating DNA in human remains. Hopefully the use of these techniques will allow a clearer picture of the racial migrations of prehistory to emerge from the present confusion of archaeological and historical speculation.

Whatever the origins of the Celts or their religious beliefs, the fact is that they were well established in most of Europe, including Britain and Ireland, for several hundred years before the Romans extended their influence to the rest of the European continent. The gods and goddesses of the Celts were numerous and, while there were shared national deities, each tribe also worshipped its own local gods or geni loci. Some authorities have attempted to classify the Celtic pantheon by type, if not locality. For instance Dr Anne Ross divides the Celtic gods into the Horned God, as stag, bull and ram, the Warrior God and The Goddesses. She also has sub-categories for the sacred cult of the head, sacred birds and divine animals (Ross 1967). This classification makes it easier to understand the complexities of the Celtic pantheon, and the role of the deities within it, but also detracts somehow from the rich and exotic multiplicity of deities represented by Celtic polytheism.

Our knowledge of the Celtic deities and the religious rituals used to honour them comes from dubious and second-hand historical sources and the presently available archaeological evidence. Before the arrival of the Romans, with their anthropomorphic god forms, there is some evidence that the Celts were reluctant to represent their gods in human form. Some stone and wooden images are found from the 6th century BCE onwards, but most of the effigies of Celtic deities in fact only date from the post-Roman period.

These later images have obviously been interpreted from a Roman perspective which only provide a vague idea of how the Celts themselves actually visualised their deities. This process continued in the historical period where we find Celtic gods and goddesses hidden in human disguise within the Arthurian legends, the lives of the saints and the collection of medieval Celtic Welsh tales of The Mabinogion.

The Romans were fairly tolerant of the other pagan belief systems they encountered in their march across Europe. They did however have an ethnocentric outlook and tended to regard the people they conquered as barbarians who followed 'barbaric rites'. The Romans treated the religious beliefs of the lands they conquered in a colonial fashion, identifying the local deities with their own gods and taking over the native cults. In this way, for instance, if they came across a Celtic warrior god they would say he was Mars, their god of war, Sun gods were usually renamed Apollo, moon goddesses were Diana and the Celtic god of the forest became Silvanus. As Romans and Celts intermarried, and a Romano-Celtic society was created, the differences between the Celtic and Roman deities became even more blurred.

The priestly caste of the Celts, as mentioned earlier, were the druids who officiated at public ceremonies, were responsible for making sacrifices and acted as lawgivers and judges. They were sub-divided into three separate grades or offices known as bards, ovates and druids. The latter were the learned men - and women, as female druids are mentioned in historical accounts of the cultus - who took the role of teachers, philosophers, lawmakers and religious administrators. In contrast the bards were story-tellers, poets and singers and the ovates took the role of seers, diviners and interpreters of sacrifices. The bardic grade was more important then it seems for several reasons. Firstly, music, song and poetry had a high profile in Celtic culture and secondly because the spiritual teachings of druidism were passed on by an oral tradition embracing songs, poetry and riddles. It was the grade of bard, combined with the role of the ovate, that survived the ideological onslaught of Christianity and preserved traditional Celtic culture and religious ideas into the Middle Ages and beyond.

The actual derivation of the word 'druid' is hotly disputed. It is generally said to originate from the Sanskrit drus, the Welsh derwydd and the Celtic derw all meaning wood, oak or tree. Early Gallic references to the druids render the word as druvid and the second part comes from the Indo-European root wid, meaning 'to know'. The druids were therefore the people of the woods and trees or, more esoterically perhaps, 'the people of the tree knowledge'. This seems to be a sensible description, considering that the druids held their religious ceremonies in a sacred grove, known as a nemeton, and used a mystical tree alphabet. Several Roman writers also mention that the oak tree was sacred to the Celts and was a symbol of one of their principal gods.

If our knowledge of Celtic religious beliefs and practices is usually obtained from second-hand sources, then what little is known about the druids emphasises this fact. The most detailed account of the druids is the famous one attributed to Julius Caesar, who encountered them during his campaigns in Gaul (France) and obviously writes from the biased viewpoint of a conqueror. He said the Gallic druids were ruled by an archdruid and when he died he was succeeded by the person second highest in the priesthood. If this person was not suitable or worthy enough for the position, or several challengers contended for the vacancy the contest was decided either by a democratic vote or, if all else failed, ritual combat.

The druids, according to Caesar, instructed the young men of the Celtic tribes in both esoteric and moral matters. They were generally consulted for advice on important issues affecting the tribe and acted as judges in family disputes and criminal cases. Caesar described an annual assembly held at a special place in Gaul regarded as the sacred centre of the country. This idea of an omphalas, or geographical sacred centre, where important religious ceremonies were held and sometimes rulers crowned is an ancient geomantic concept. It will be returned to later in the book in the story of St Patrick's challenge to the Irish druids at Tara, the sacred centre of Ireland.

In his description of Gallic druidism Caesar repeats the popular belief of the time that the cultus originated in Britain and was exported to the rest of Celtic Europe. He mentions the idea in slightly sceptical terms, but says the druids of Gaul believed their institution (sic) was devised in Britain. Caesar goes on to say that the Gallic druids visited these islands for the purpose of studying their beliefs in their original form. This statement has been credited to Caesar's chief informant, Diviciacus, who it is believed was actually a member of the druid order (Spence 1949). The training period for a novice druid was apparently twenty years and, as mentioned earlier, druidic teachings were given orally. Caesar states that a central doctrine of druidic philosophy was the belief that 'souls do not suffer death, but pass from one body to another.' This idea, and the Celtic belief in the immortality of the soul, has been taken to mean that the druids accepted reincarnation. However, some authorities doubt this proposition and claim, rather unconvincingly I feel, that the idea mentioned by Caesar is a reference to shape shifting (Ross 1967). Other writers assert the Celts believed the soul passed from its physical shell to another, spirit, body in the underworld (Piggott 1968).

It is Caesar who provides the only description of the alleged druidic method of human sacrifice known as 'the wicker man', although his account was copied by other writers giving it a possibly spurious authenticity. Caesar claims that criminals and prisoners-of-war were herded into giant wickerwork figures and these were then set alight by the druids. This horrific description of mass human sacrifice has sadly become one of the most potent images of druidism and still survives today. It formed the melodramatic, if exciting, climax to the 1970s British movie The Wicker Man, starring Edward Woodward, Christopher Lee and Britt Eckland, and based on the novel by Robert Hardy and Anthony Schaeffer.

Caesar was certainly not an unbiased observer or chronicler and, for political and ethnocentric reasons, wanted to paint the druids as black as possible. He was supported, no doubt for similar reasons, by other classical writers such as Tacitus, who described the druid altars soaked with the blood of captured prisoners and the Celtic priests divining the future from their entrails.

Lucan also described the forest sanctuaries used by the druids in blood chilling terms. He said: 'There were many dark springs running there and grim-faced figures of gods, uncouthly hewn from untrimmed tree trunks, rooting to whiteness.' It is all spooky stuff and no doubt had the desired effect on the cultured urbanites of Rome who read Lucan's accounts.

It is probable, even highly possible, that while these accounts were exaggerated they did also contain a substantial element of truth. I have no wish to whitewash or sanitise the ancient pagan cultures by imposing modern, politically correct views on their actions. Animal and human sacrifice did exist in pre-Christian times and, as the Old Testament indicates, sacrificial offerings were even a prominent aspect of the Hebrew religion and, of course, Christianity has Judaic roots. The sacrificial aspects of Judeo-Christianity, influenced it must be said by ancient paganism, still survive in a sublimated form in the Christian Mass.

It is therefore conceivable that the druids practised sacrifices and the archaeological evidence from Celtic sites offers support for this idea. If widespread or mass human sacrifices were carried out, and this is more debatable, they must be considered within the wider historical context of human society, and its religious beliefs, at that time. It should also be noted that Caesar's sensational account of the druids and their practices contrasts with those of less biased Greek writers, who compared the Celtic priesthood favourably with the Persian magi, the Egyptian high priests, the Hindu Brahmins and the disciples of Pythagoras.

Pliny also has provided one of the few descriptions of a druidic ceremony, but without the bloodcurdling imagery of Lucan or Caesar. This is his famous account of the ritual cutting of the mistletoe by the archdruid in the sacred grove. He tells us this plants was sacred to the Celts because it grew on the oak tree. The druids, he claimed, would not perform any of their ceremonies unless they were near an oak or at least had a branch of the tree laying on their altars. The oak was not, of course, only sacred to the Celts for the Romans, and other Indo-European races venerated it as a sacred tree associated with the thunder god.

The druids called the mistletoe by a Celtic name meaning 'all heal' and they ritually cut it from the oak tree on the sixth day of the moon, which is presumably six days from new moon. Two white bulls were brought into the grove and a white robed druid climbed the tree armed with a ritual golden sickle. When he cut the mistletoe another druid standing below the tree caught it in his cloak so it did not touch the ground. The bulls were then sacrificed and prayers were offered to the oak god, asking him to grant the healing powers of the plant to whoever needed it.

Pliny says the druids used mistletoe in healing potions and believed it could cure sterility, was an antidote for all poisons and a general cure-all. A few years ago it was reported that Swiss doctors were researching mistletoe as a possible cure for cancer. Folklorists have pointed out that the round, white mistletoe berries resemble drops of semen and, in using magical law of sympathetic correspondence, this is why it was considered a treatment for fertility problems. The old custom of kissing under the mistletoe may also be linked with this concept.

Other writers have seen the mistletoe as the 'silver branch', the equivalent in the Celtic tradition of the famous 'golden bough' of early Roman lore. This symbolic prize was fought over in ritual combat by Rex Nemorensis, or the King of the Woods, and any challenger who wanted to usurp his place as sacred king of the grove and consort of the Goddess. The pagan symbolism of the mistletoe was not eradicated by the new religion and in fact its potency lingers on. Mistletoe is still the only traditional Christmas greenery that is not allowed to be used to decorate churches.

It is difficult from the scant evidence we have about them to say definitely that the druids inherited or adopted the earlier religious beliefs of the Megalithic and Bronze Age folk. We can however have our suspicions and make some calculated speculations. The accounts of ancient druidry were filtered through an historical lens obscured by prejudice and modern, revivalist druidism, in direct contrast, is surrounded in an aura of middle-class respectability, historical forgery and plain fantasy. Despite these two extremes there is the feeling that the real Celtic druids had inherited a far older, more shamanic, form of religion then could be found in the sophisticated classical religions of the post -Roman period. The Romans may have had their own good reasons for presenting the Celts and their priesthood as 'barbarians'. Perhaps this was partly because in their contact with druidry the comparatively sophisticated Romans found themselves face to face with an older faith. One which only survived in a very sublimated form within their own religious belief system.

In speculating about the shamanic, pre-Celtic influences in druidism, it is interesting to read the contemporary description of the chief druid at the court of an Irish Celtic king. He is described as wearing the hide of a bull, an head-dress with a speckled white bird attached with fluttering wings and a multi-coloured cloak. This sounds suspiciously like the ritual costume of a shaman.

In legendary accounts the druids are said to be able to shape shift and control the elemental forces to raise winds and create mists. Again this suggests the magical powers associated with the shamans of other cultures and time periods. How, or even whether, this image can be reconciled with modern pagan revivalists attempting to create forms of 'Celtic shamanism' is another story. It certainly provides food for thought, especially when compared with the 'magical' activities of the Celtic saints, who, as we shall see later in this book, seem to have inherited the druidic arts of wizardry.

So far the history and background of the Celtic pagan religion in pre-Roman Britain and Europe has been discussed, but in the 1st century CE the British Celts - if that rather loose and rather generalised description can be applied to them - faced two new threats. One was military and cultural and came from the Roman legions who invaded southern Britain with an estimated 50,000 troops in 43 CE. The second invasion was more subtle and it took several hundred years to achieve its objectives of conquest. This second invasion was, of course, Christianity and while the Romans finally left Britain the Christians remained, survived and flourished.

The historical and spiritual rise of early Christianity, from its humble beginnings as an obscure sect in a minor Roman colony to it becoming the official religion of that Empire and a world faith replacing the old pagan religions, is complex and complicated. As with most historical events, especially those involving religious themes, it is likely to be open to individual interpretation, prejudice and bias. How Christianity specifically is considered in the grand plan of things will depend very much on how the individual sees the central character in the Christian story, Joshua be Joseph, or, to give him his Greek name, Jesus.

Obviously a conventional Christian will see Jesus in a totally orthodox way as the promised messiah born of a virgin, the God Incarnate, who died on the cross to cleanse humanity's sin, died, was resurrected on the third day and rose to Heaven to sit at the right hand of God. Unfortunately for Christian orthodoxy, although they try to ignore the fact most of the time, this image is a surprisingly pagan one. It owes more to Middle Eastern myths about sun gods and vegetation-saviour gods, who sacrifice themselves in a ritualistic death to bring fertility to the land, dwell in the underworld and are then reborn, than it does to the historical Jesus.

One of the reasons why the pagans eventually accepted Christianity, after a prolonged struggle, was their recognition of Jesus as a sacred king and divine victim. He was another version of the saviour god who was sacrificed for the good of the people and was then reborn in the spring. Where there was a conflict between the Christianity and the pagan Old Religion was the insistence of the Church that it possessed a spiritual monopoly on spiritual experience and religious observance. In the view of the Christian priests worship should only be given to the monotheistic tribal god Yahweh or Jehovah of the Old Testament and all other gods were false idols and devils.

An alternative view of Jesus, supported by the information in the Gospels, presents him as an ordinary man, in fact a political rebel, who claimed descent from the Royal House of David. In this version he takes the role of the promised messiah of the Old Testament and deliberately sets out to overthrow the Roman occupation army and its Jewish quislings who rule Judea. It has been pointed out that Jesus was executed for stirring up sedition and rebellion and for claiming to be King of the Jews. He had attacked the temple in Jerusalem and when he was arrested he was accompanied by armed followers. At his hearing before Pilate, Jesus was not condemned to be stoned as a heretic, as later happened to his (twin?) brother James, but to death on the cross with a criminal and a political rebel.

Another alternative, or complimentary, image of Jesus the man represents him as one of the many 'wandering rabbis', or spiritual teachers, of the period whose self-proclaimed mission was to reform what they saw as the decadence of Judaism. In this scenario Jesus taught the mysteries of 'the kingdom of God within' to his inner circle of disciples, while preaching a watered down version of his teachings to the masses. Obviously this image of Jesus as a religious reformer and heretical rabbi is not acceptable to orthodox Christians. They prefer to accept the, blatantly, pagan version of the mythical Christ, from the Greek Christos or 'Anointed One', as the 'Son of God'.

There is little evidence to suggest Jesus believed he was preaching a universal message to humankind. Instead he seems to be preaching a reformed version of Judaism tailored to the immediate needs of the Chosen People in the situation they found themselves in during the first half of the 1st century. In The Gospel of Matthew, Jesus clearly told his disciples not to attempt to convert the Gentiles but instead preach their message to 'the lost sheep of Israel.' As we shall see later, this commandment was twisted and misrepresented to justify Paul's missions to Asia Minor, Rome and Western Europe. In fact the teachings offered by Jesus were not designed for the Gentiles (pagans), but for those Jews who had strayed from their own faith.

The original 'Christian Church' founded immediately after the crucifixion was a Jewish sect. Its members were referred to as the Nazarenes and were led by Jacob or James, the brother of Jesus. The Nazarenes accepted Jesus as the promised messiah of the Old Testament but still regarded themselves as part of the Judaic religion, even if the orthodox Jews in turn regarded them as heretics. They had no desire to convert the Gentiles and, like many early Christian sects, did not regard Jesus as the Son of God or God Incarnate. Such concepts were alien to the Jewish religious tradition and were introduced later into Christianity from the pagan religions (Berresford-Ellis 1985).

Paul at first persecuted the Nazarenes but after a dramatic conversion he became a convert to the sect. Unfortunately he developed heretical beliefs claiming Jesus had been divine and his message was a universal one for the whole of humankind. These extreme views led him into conflict with the other members and a split developed. Paul had gathered a following of ex-pagans and eventually he and his disciples broke away from the Nazarenes. He travelled to Asia Minor to preach his own version of the Christian message, claiming without foundation that he had the support of the Nazarene leaders such as James, John and Peter.. He justified this schism from the Nazarenes by claiming that, while Peter had been entrusted with preaching the gospel to the Jews by Jesus, he (Paul) had received a direct revelation from Christ to reveal 'the good news' to the pagan Gentiles.

Faced with the threat from Paul the Nazarenes retaliated by sending out their own missionaries For ten years the struggle went on between Paul's band of 'Gentile Christians' and the 'Jewish Christians' represented by the Nazarene sect in Jerusalem. This power struggle came to a climax when, in 67 CE, the Emperor Nero moved to crush the Jewish revolts against Roman rule. After Nero's death in 69 his successor, Vespasian, continued the campaign and his troops managed to recapture Jerusalem. According to the historian Josephus, the Jewish high priest of Jerusalem seized the opportunity to eliminate the heretical Nazarenes who not only opposed Roman rule but his own authority. James, and some of the other Nazarene leaders, were brought before a Jewish court, charged with heresy and blasphemy and stoned to death. The sect managed to survive this event, until in the year 90 the Nazarenes were officially prohibited from practising and teaching their Jewish heresy.

With the death of James the way was left open for Paul to consolidate his power base and extend the influence of his version of Christianity without any serious opposition from rival groups. He did this by baptising Gentiles throughout the Roman Empire and establishing churches with bishops and priests. Eventually this was to culminate in the 4th century acceptance of Pauline Christianity as the official religion of the Roam Empire and the rise of the bishop of Rome as the supreme pontiff ruling over Christendom.

Along the way the new Churchainity adopted many more pagan beliefs including the seasonal festivals of the pagan religious calendar. Early Christian converts, faced with pressure from their rulers, peers and missionaries accepted an unhistorical image of Jesus. One borrowed from pagan myths which depicted him as the sacrificial divine king, born of a virgin at the winter solstice and ritually killed and reborn in the spring.

At first Christianity was only one of many exotic new cults striving to attract spiritual consumers in the 1st and 2nd centuries CE. While the so-called barbarians - the Celts, Germanic tribes and Norse people - seemed to have been content with their versions of paganism, the bored and decadent inhabitants of the classical world were seeking religious variety in alternative forms of spirituality. These included Oriental cults and the so-called 'mystery religions' or Mysteries, open only to a selected elite of initiates in their most sophisticated forms but originally the mass pagan celebrations of the people. The famous Eleusinian Mysteries in Greece, for instance, probably originated around 1800 BCE when the local families, dedicated to the service of the early version of the goddess Demeter, practised magical rites to increase the fertility of the land and the harvest (D'Alviella 1981).

The two major mystery religions imported from the Middle East that were to separately challenge Christianity were the cults of Mithras and Isis. Mithraism has been described as 'the Freemasonry of the Roman world' (Godwin 1981), because it was an all-male cult that spread as a secret fraternity throughout the imperial army. It originated in the early dualistic religious beliefs of ancient Persia (Iran) and early Christianity borrowed extensively from it to produce its acceptable 'pagan' image of Jesus. Mithras was the result of a virgin birth and was born in a cave attended by shepherds around December 25th. In the dualistic Persian religion, Mithras is a type of sun god of light and battles with the evil Ahriman, representing the powers of darkness. Godwin (1981) says that Ahriman is misrepresented as the principle of evil. In common with most pagan gods of darkness, he in fact represents an unknowable or higher level of, possibly elder, gods who exist outside time and space. This interpretation illustrates the fundamental difference between pagan and Christian concepts of dualism and between the old gods of the underworld and the Church's concept of the Devil or Satan.

Mithras dies a sacrificial death but is reborn and at the end of the world will fight a final battle with the forces of evil leading to his triumphant victory. The central icon of the Mithraic faith is the sacrificial slaying of the cosmic bull, whose blood flows into the ground, fertilizes the earth and brings creation into existence. The rituals of Mithraism were performed in underground cave sanctuaries and, in common with other mystery cults, its initiation rituals involved a baptism, a death and rebirth enactment and a ritual meal. These elements were later adopted by the early Christian Church.

Mithraism was essentially a soldier's cult and support for it extended through the ranks and to the highest levels. Even the Emperors openly supported it as an official imperial cultus and this lasted until the early 4th century, when Emperor Constantine the Great switched his support to the new religion of Christianity. There seems to have been a revival of the cult between 357 and 387 by pagan Roman senators, who were followers of the Emperor Julian Apostate. He briefly tried to revive the old pagan ways but with the collapse of the power of Imperial Rome the cult of Mithras seems to have slipped into historical obscurity. A Christian church was built over the last Mithraic underground shrine in Rome.

The other mystery cult to have a significant impact on early Christianity was the worship of Isis, As is the case today among many occultists and neo- pagans, Egypt in the 1st and 2nd centuries CE was regarded as a source of magic and arcane wisdom. It was therefore almost predictable that the cult of Isis should sweep across the Roman empire and even reach the British Isles. Similarities between the Egyptian religion of Isis and Osiris and Christianity are obvious. Osiris is a vegetation god betrayed by his twin brother Set (a Judas figure) and killed. He is reborn and then rules as the god of the underworld. Isis, the moon goddess, is an archetypal mother figure in some of her aspects. She is the pagan Great Mother Goddess and images of her suckling Horus, the sun god, are almost identical to the medieval statues of the Virgin Mary cradling the baby Jesus. Catholic images of the Madonna wearing a blue robe and a crown of stars and standing on a crescent moon would be easily recognised and accepted by any Ancient Egyptian or Roman citizen as Isis.

It was against this general background of religious diversity, spiritual experimentation and socio-cultural upheaval that the Roman invasion of Britain occurred in 43 CE. Although, as noted earlier, the Romans were fairly tolerant of other pagan beliefs they did persecute druidism throughout the Empire. This was because it was regarded as a political force responsible for organising Celtic resistance to Roman rule. Christianity was persecuted by the Romans for similar reasons. The occupation of Britain was resisted by some local Celtic leaders and the druids were actively involved in the organisation and support of this resistance and in the subsequent uprisings.

The most dramatic example recorded of this druidic resistance came in north Wales. In 60 CE, the new Roman governor appointed by Nero, called Gaius Suetonius Paulinus, marched with contingents of the 14th and 20th legions on Ynys Mon or Anglesey as it was renamed in Saxon times, the Isle of the Angles. The island had become a national symbol and centre for Celtic resistance against the Romans, sheltering thousands of refugees from other parts of Wales and a large community of druids. Paulinus knew he had to capture it if Roman rule was to be permanently established in the west of Britain.

The Roman legions approached Anglesey from the south and flat bottomed boats were used to ferry the troops across the Menai Straits to the shores of the island. The Roman historian Tacitus says the soldiers were led by cavalry, who swam in the water beside their horses. Little could have prepared them for the sight that greeted them as they waded towards the shore. Tacitus says: 'The enemy lined the shore in a dense armed mass. Among them were black robed women with dishevelled hair like Furies, brandishing torches. Close by stood the druids, raising their arms to heaven and screaming dreadful curses.'

Tacitus says that at first the Roman legionaries were paralysed by fear and horror. They stood still, making them an easy target for the Celts lined up on the shore. It seemed as if the battle would be lost before it began, but the Roman general and his officers urged the soldiers to advance, telling them not to be afraid of the Celtic women or the druids' curses. Spurred on by their officers the legionaries advanced in tight battle formation. Shield to shield they swept through the ranks of the women and the Celtic warriors 'enveloping them in the flames of their own torches.' The druids and the 'black robed women' - who were probably female druids or at least Celtic priestesses of some kind - were put to the sword. The druidic altars were overturned and broken and the sacred groves were cut down. Effectively the power of the druids in north Wales was ruthlessly smashed by this bloody massacre.

Evidence of these events on Anglesey were uncovered when the RAF station was built at Valley on the island. Bulldozers uncovered several artefacts, including a chain with five neck rings, possibly a slave collar, bronze ornaments and even the remains of several chariots. It has been speculated that this was one of the druidic sites sacked by the Romans. The objects may even have been sacrificial offerings made to the Old Gods to invoke their assistance to defeat the Roman legions. (Cottrell 1958).

It would be over two hundred and fifty years before Christianity became accepted as the official religion of the Roman Empire but, as will be described in the next chapter, the first Christian converts may have already arrived in Britain.

Chapter Two
Early Christianity in Roman Britain

The Christian faith had reached Rome by 60 CE, when Paul arrived to preach his version of Christianity. It is therefore fairly safe to speculate that were a few practising Christians, or at least those who practised both Christian and pagan beliefs, among the first legionaries to arrive in Britain in the twenty years after the Roman invasion. By the end of the 1st century BCE the leadership of the Roman (Catholic) Church was led by a Bishop Clement and he was responsible for putting forward the doctrine of apostolic succession. This doctrine was eventually to transform the bishopric of Rome into the papacy as it was known in the Middle Ages. By the 3rd century Christianity was 'one of the major religions of the Graeco-Roman world' (Frend 1984) although, as we saw in Chapter One, it had to struggle against other rivals including Mithraism, the cultus of Isis, the classical Mysteries and, later, Gnosticism.

The earliest stories relating to the arrival of Christianity in Britain are legendary accounts of doubtful origin and providence. They appear to have been written down by monkish chroniclers, who were less then unbiased observers and recorders of historical events, and many of these accounts were designed to provide a unique pedigree and authority for British Christianity. One of these stories claims that St Paul himself visited Britain and founded churches with priests and bishops. This tale is to be found in the so-called *Sonnini Manuscript*, allegedly a translation of a Greek document in the archives at Constantinople (Istanbul). This manuscript may have been a medieval forgery and it tells how when Paul visited Spain he heard that one of the lost tribes of Israel had settled in Britain.

Paul left Spain and took a ship to Armorica (Brittany). From there he landed on the south coast of Roman Britain. When the apostle arrived he was allegedly greeted by large crowds who led him to Londonium (London) and there he found lodgings with a fellow Hebrew. While in the city Paul preached the gospel at Mount Lud and may of those who heard his words were converted. Ludgate in the City of London, originally the Gate of Lugh, is near to the present site of St Paul's cathedral. In Roman times the cathedral was a temple dedicated to the classical moon goddess Diana.

The manuscript goes on to say that 'certain of the druids' came to Paul in private and they showed him by their rites and ceremonies that they were descended from the Israelites. Paul seems to have accepted this and, according to the manuscript, gave the druids the 'kiss of peace'. He stayed in London for three months preaching the gospel before sailing back across the Channel to Gaul. There he preached to the Roman garrisons and the Celtic tribe of the Belgae before travelling back to Asia Minor. (Williams 1970).

In addition to this rather dubious source, Paul's visit to Britain is mentioned in the writings of several early churchmen including Irenaeus, Tertullian, Origen, Eusebus and Athanasius. Theodoret, Bishop of Cyprus, writing in the 5th century says: ' Paul, liberated from his first captivity at Rome, preached the gospel to the Britons and others in the West..the Britons and the Cymry (Welsh).' Clement claimed that Paul visited 'the utmost bounds of the West', which was Britain. Cappellus in his History of the Apostles says Paul preached in every European country including Britain.

This story was eagerly seized upon by such religious sects as the British Israelites who believed the Celts were a lost tribe of Israel and the British were the second 'chosen people'. This concept influenced the 18th and 19th century druidic revivals and had its followers among right-wing political groups who used it to support British imperialism. Paul's visit to Britain also had its supporters in the Roman Church. The Morning Post in Match 1931 reported that a group of English mayors had met with Pope Pius XI and he had expressed his opinion that Paul introduced Christianity to Britain.

There are also some odd references to a disciple of Paul called Aristobulus the Aged, or in Welsh Arwysti Hen, who is described by some clerical writers as a British bishop and the brother of St Barnabas. It is alleged he travelled to Britain from Rome and suffered martyrdom here. In one version Aristobulus was chosen by Paul to be a missionary bishop and sent to Britain to convert the Celts. He is alleged to have built churches and ordained priests before he was martyred.

One of the alleged companions of Aristobulus was Bran the Blessed or Bran Vendigaeth, the father of the Celtic rebel king Caradoc the Pendragon or 'High Chief' of the British tribes (He should not be confused with the Irish Bran the Blessed who was buried at Tower Hill in London). Caradoc had been defeated by the Romans and taken to Rome in chains as a slave. When he was eventually released his father and his daughter, Gladys, remained in Rome as hostages for his good behaviour. Gladys married the Roman Commander-in-Chief of Britain. It is said the two captives converted to Christianity and Bran returned home and persuaded many of the British Celts to accept the new religion.

The most famous account of the arrival of early Christianity and the establishment of the British church by Joseph of Arimathea, the great-uncle of Jesus, in either 35 or 63 CE - depending on which version you read. This story was regarded as very important by the Celtic Church as they believed it established a direct link between Jesus and the foundation of Christianity in Britain. Joseph is mention in Matthew's gospel as 'a rich man' and one of Jesus' disciples He was also a member of the Jewish priesthood. After the crucifixion he went to Pilate and begged him to release the body of Jesus into his care. He then wrapped the body in a clean linen cloth and placed it in his own private tomb. He rolled a great stone across the entrance to seal it while Mary, mother of Jesus, and Mary Magdelene sat outside. (Matthew 28:57-61) In Mark 15:42-43, Joseph is described as 'an honourable counsellor, which (sic) also waited for the Kingdom of God' and Luke 23:50-51 refers to him as 'a good and just man'. John 19:38 describes Joseph as a 'secret disciple' because he feared the orthodox Jews. This term 'secret disciple' may in fact refer to the inner circle of initiates around Jesus who were personally instructed in the doctrine of the 'Kingdom of God within'.

Following the disappearance of body of Jesus from the tomb there was a widespread persecution of the early Judeo-Christian Church (or Nazarenes). In the apocryphal Gospel of Nicodemus it says attempts were made to arrest Joseph. He only outwitted his pursuers and escaped to his home city of Arimathea with angelic help. Joseph then became a disciple of the apostle Philip and was appointed to attend the Virgin Mary and was present when she died. In some accounts he became the legal guardian or foster-father of Jesus after Mary's husband died. Here the story becomes vague and it is unclear whether Philip asked Joseph to go on a missionary visit to Britain or Joseph was forced to flee abroad to escape further persecution. Esoteric traditions claim he was invited to the British Isles by the druids.

In the legendary accounts Joseph, Mary Magdalene and her brother Lazarus, take ship to southern France, where Mary and Lazarus decided to stay, while Joseph travelled on to Britain with a small group of his followers. Some versions say Joseph arrived in North Wales and was briefly imprisoned. In other accounts he and his companions sailed directly to Glastonbury or, as it was known in Celtic times, Ynys Wtrin (the Glass Island). In those days Glastonbury was virtually an island surrounded by the sea and marshes so Joseph's party could easily have achieved this feat of navigation.

Glastonbury was an important sacred centre for centuries before Joseph arrived. In the 3rd century BCE the Celts had established lake villages at Glastonbury and nearby Meare. There is a local legend that a stone circle once stood on top of Glastonbury Tor and there is also evidence of a ritual maze circling around the hill, possibly dating from the druidic period or even earlier. The Celts regarded the Tor as one of the entrances to Annwn, the underworld, ruled by Gwynn ap Nudd, the god of the dead. He was also the leader of the Wild Hunt and rode out of the hollow hill of the Tor on winter nights with his pack of hell hounds to hunt human souls. In the popular legends associated with Joseph of Arimathea's settlement in Glastonbury the pagan significance and symbolism of the area became intermixed with Christian myth. In some cases it is difficult to know where one ends and the other begins.

The Joseph legend says that his visit to Glastonbury was not the first time he had travelled to Britain. In Cornish folklore Joseph is known as a 'tin man' or a wealthy merchant who traded with the tin-miners of Cornwall. This legend goes further to say that on one of his trading trips Joseph was accompanied by the boy Jesus. This charming story formed the basis for William Blake's famous poem and hymn Jerusalem. In esoteric tradition it is even said Jesus actually studied with the druids and was initiated into their inner mysteries.

It is know that Phoenician and Greek traders visited Cornwall and West Wales in search of tin and in 350 BC Aristotle referred to Britain as 'the Tin Island' . The Western sea routes had been used since the Bronze Age by traders from various parts of Europe. These ancient sea routes linked north-east Ireland with the Isle of Man and Scotland, southern Ireland with North and West Wales and all these areas with northern Cornwall. These sea routes were not isolated trading links but also connected with a network of prehistoric trackways criss-crossing Wales, southern England and the West Country. In the Roman period one famous route led from St David's in south-west Wales, across the Preseli hills to Carmarthen, across South Wales to the River Severn and then through the Celtic/Roman city of Bath to London, Canterbury and the short sea route to Gaul. In the 5th and 6th centuries these ancient sea and land routes were extensively used by Celtic Christian missionaries in their travels preaching the gospel.

If Joseph had travelled to Britain previously it would explain why he made directly for Glastonbury on his last trip. He and his twelve companions (making the mystical thirteen of lunar mythology and folklore) landed in Glastonbury at Wearyall Hill, just south-west of the modern town, overlooking the Somerset marshes. In the legend Joseph planted his staff into the ground on the hill and it miraculously took root and flowered into a thorn three, This Holy Thorn still flowers in Glastonbury at various religious sites in the town around the midwinter solstice.

Frances Howard-Gordon (1982) has pointed out that the hawthorn was sacred to the Celts, and probably earlier peoples, and was a symbol of the Goddess in her maiden aspect. In folklore it is associated with fertility and spring rites like May Day, the Celtic Beltane, to encourage the growth of vegetation and celebrate the coming of summer. This connection with fertility is remembered in a local Somerset saying which goes: 'If St Joseph's Day is clear, we shall get a fertile year.' It was considered unlucky to pick hawthorn or display it in the house and similar folklore is associated with the Holy Thorn at Glastonbury. When a 17th century Puritan tried to chop down the thorn on Wearyall Hill he was blinded by a flying piece of wood from the trunk.

When Joseph reached Glastonbury he was met by the local tribal king called Arviragus and he was quite an important figure in British history at the time. He was the Prince of Kernow (Cornwall) and the son of King Cunobelinus,'The Hound of Bel'. Arivagus was also the cousin of the Celtic warlord Caradoc and joined forces with him to resist the Roman occupation in 43 CE. When Joseph arrived the king seemed not to be interested in the new religion the saint had to offer. Arviragus did however took pity on the party of weary travellers and allowed them to stay. In fact William of Malmesbury, writing in the 13th century, says Arviragus and three other pagan kings in the area granted Joseph twelve hides of land in Glastonbury. A hide was approximately one hundred and sixty acres. This tax free-land, the so-called 'Twelve Hides of Glastonbury', is referred to in the Domesday Book of 1087 and it was also a matter of dispute between the Celtic and Roman Churches.

In 1409 France and Spain disputed the primacy of the British Church. They had to retract after it was accepted that St Joseph had founded the first Christian settlement in Britain on these famous twelve hides of land. This original Christian foundation also seems to have been accepted by Augustine who, according to William of Malmesbury, wrote to Pope Gregory telling him of the establishment of an ancient Christian community in 'the western confines of Britain' with a church dedicated to the Blessed Virgin Mary.

The church or chapel mentioned by Augustine was built by Joseph in 37 or 38 on a site at the base of the Tor after the Archangel Gabriel appeared to him in a dream. This early chapel was of mud-and-wattle, probably had a thatched roof and had the same dimensions as the Judaic Tabernacle. The first British Christian converts were baptised by Joseph and hermits worshipped at the chapel until the 5th century, when it is said St Patrick established a monastic community at Glastonbury.

In 630 Paulinus, one of the missionaries who came over with Augustine, preserved the chapel by encasing it in lead and a stone church was built around it. This survived the 8th century establishment of a Saxon abbey by the Roman Church on the site but was destroyed in 1184, when a great fire swept through Glastonbury Abbey. A Christian community survived At Glastonbury until the medieval abbey was destroyed in the Reformation. On the orders of Henry VIII, the last abbot was executed on the Tor.

Several writers have claimed that the Twelve Hides of Glastonbury and the dimensions of St Mary's Chapel have an occult (hidden) significance. It has even been claimed that the ground plan of the New Jerusalem described by St John the Divine can be found at Glastonbury (Michell 1972 and 1983). It is interesting that John had an important significance to the Celtic Church. The Celts, and the peoples before them, were Goddess worshippers and it is not too difficult to see in 'Our Lady of Glastonbury' a Christianised version of the Great Mother of the Celtic pantheon. In the Jewish Cabbala the Archangel Gabriel is said to be the planetary angel of the moon. As is known, the moon goddess had a prominent role in the pagan Old Religion and its post-Christian survivals.

Possibly the most extraordinary legend associated with Joseph is that he brought the Holy Grail to Glastonbury and it is buried either in the Abbey grounds or under the Tor. In Christian mythology the Grail was the cup used at the Last Supper, although the legend of the Grail, or more correctly the Cauldron, actually date back to pre-Christian times. The Grail tradition at Glastonbury seems to date from the Middle Ages and may have originated with the High History of the Holy Grail compiled from The Book of Josephes, Joseph's son. This story seems to be a bizarre attempt to provide a Jewish ancestry for Arthur and his knights and distance the Grail legend from its pagan roots. In fact, as we shall see, many of the Welsh saints were allegedly related to Arthur and other characters in the Arthurian legends.

Considering the legend of Joseph and the Grail, it is interesting to note that on Chalice Hill, in the shadow of the Tor, is the famous Chalice Well. This was originally a pre-Christian sacred spring and the occultist Dion Fortune describes it as 'The Blood Spring'. She says it was oriented to the midsummer solstice and was a druidic site of sacrifice. It was also guarded by Morgan Le Fay, the dark sorceress and half-sister of Arthur who lived on Chalice Hill with her nine priestesses.(Fortune 1971). In

Welsh myth, as described in The Spoils of Annwn, the pagan Cauldron is guarded by nine maidens and is captured by Arthur who ventures into the Celtic underworld. It is tempting to speculate that Joseph baptised his first Christian converts at this ancient sacred spring.

Joseph died in 90 CE and was buried at Glastonbury, 'the holiest erthe in England'. His death is mention in Maelgwyn of Avalon's Historia de Rebus Brittanicis dating from 540. He says: 'The Isle of Avalon, greedy of burials, received thousands of sleepers, among them Joseph of Marmore from Arimathea by name, entered his perpetual sleep' The tomb of Joseph was allegedly carved with the epitaph ' Ad Brittanos Veri Post Christum Sepelivi. Dociu, Quievi' 'I came to Britain after burying Christ. I taught. I rested.' The bodies of Joseph and his companions were allegedly unearthed in the Middle Ages by monks from Glastonbury Abbey.

After Joseph's death the Grail was either buried somewhere in Glastonbury or passed to his son Josephes. He passed it on to his cousin, Alain, the son of Bron, who passed it to his brother Josue. After this the role of hereditary Grail keeper was taken by six kings, the last of whom was Pelles. His son was Sir Galahad of the Round Table who has a special position in the Grail legends. Various guardians of the Grail have been claimed since Arthurian times, including the medieval monks of Glastonbury Abbey itself and the heretical Order of Knight Templars.

After Joseph there are references to several missionaries from the Glastonbury Christian community visiting other countries to preach the gospel. The next, legendary, account of Christianity reaching these islands dates from the end of the 2nd century CE. In 185 King Lucius or Lucian, known as Llewrwg to his Celtic subjects, allegedly wrote to Pope Eleutherius (177-192) and asked him to send Christian missionaries to Britain. Two missionaries were duly sent, SS Fagan and Dyfan. Their purpose was to instruct the king and his people in the Christian religion and 'consecrate such churches as had been dedicated to divers false gods to the honour of the true God.'

The mission by the two saints is briefly mentioned in a few lines by the medieval monkish chronicler Bede and it is linked with Glastonbury, where it is said Fagan and Dyfan carried on the Christian tradition started by Joseph. The Glastonbury cycle of legends also link Lucius with the Chalice Well and the Tor. It suggests the king was already a Christian when he made is request to the Pope and had been baptised in 137 at Chalice Well. It is also said Lucius built the original church dedicated to St Michael on the Tor in 167. If this story is true, then it must have been there when the Celtic saint Collen had his close encounter with Gwynn ap Nudd several hundred years later.

It has been alleged that as a result of Lucius's request and the Roman mission four nation-wide Christian centres were established at Glastonbury, Gloucester, London and Llandaff. St Peter's church at Cornhill in the City of London is supposed to have been founded by Lucius. He made it the metropolitan church of the kingdom until it was superseded by Canterbury following the 6th century mission by Augustine. When Lucius died he was buried at Gloucester and this suggests he may have been a Romano-British tribal king ruling the West Country or the Welsh border area.

In considering the story of Lucius it should be remembered that at the period he was allegedly mass converting the Celtic tribes southern Britain had been occupied by the Romans for over hundred years. There is also little archaeological evidence, so far, to suggest Britain at this time had a large Christian population sustaining many churches and religious centres. It seems more likely that the story, with its specific mention of a Catholic take-over at Glastonbury, was invented at a later date to provide the Roman Church with an early presence in Britain and authority over the British Celtic Church founded by Joseph.

The earliest archaeological evidence for Christian worship in Britain dates from the end of the 3rd century. This evidence probably comes from wealthy Roman families who became Christian converts before leaving Rome to travel to the colonies. These people would have been military personnel, traders or members of the Roman civil service. Tertullion, writing at this period, claimed: 'The extremities of Spain, to various parts of Gaul, the regions of Britain which have never been penetrated by Roman arms have received the religion of Christ.' Such claims made by biased sources need to be treated with caution. The evidence suggests early forms of Christian worship were only found in the areas of Roman occupied Britain now known as southern England, parts of East Anglia, the North Country and south-east Wales. Cornwall, West and North Wales and Scotland were largely untouched by the first wave of Christian belief (Watts 1991)

Even where early Christianity had become established in the Roman Empire it had little political power. It faced persecution from successive Emperors who believed the new religion challenged Roman religious beliefs, the state and their own divine authority as supreme rulers. Christianity was regarded with suspicion because it was seen as politically subversive,in the sense it was a threat to the status quo. By the 3rd century Christian believers had reached prominent positions in Roman society and the Emperors feared its doctrines might influence the ruling classes and threaten the imperial power base.

It was during one of the periods when the Christians were being persecuted that the most famous British martyr, St Alban, suffered his fate. In 189 a North African called Septimus Severus became Emperor and began a program to eradicate Christianity from the Empire. Troops under his command where active in Gaul where they put to death the bishop of Lughduneses (Lyon). Severus apparently crossed the Channel to Britain to put down a mutiny by the Celtic tribes who had allied to Rome. In 209 he led his legions north to fight back the invading Picts and, according to Bede, built an earthwork wall with a wooden palisade and towers across the Scottish border 'from sea to sea' to keep the Pictish tribes at bay.

It was on his journey north that Severus fatefully stopped at Verulanium, the modern St Albans in Hertfordshire. He asked if there were any Christians in the locality and ordered any that his troops found to be hunted down and killed. One of the Christians pursued by the imperial troops was a priest and he sought refuge in the home of a prominent Roman citizen called Albanus or Alban. It was said that when the priest arrived Alban was still a practising pagan, but he was so impressed by the man's piety that he renounced his previous beliefs and became a Christian.

Word reached the Emperor that the priest was hiding in Alban's house and he sent a detachment of soldiers to arrest him When the legionaries smashed their way into the house they found Alban dressed in the priest's robes and, thinking he was their quarry, they arrested him. Alban was brought before Severus and his real identity was quickly established. At first the Emperor was puzzled that such a high-ranking Roman official as Alban should have given sanctuary to a subversive on the run from the authorities. He bluntly asked Alban to explain why he had helped someone who had insulted the pagan gods by not worshipping them, and who followed a false religion worshipping a man who was crucified as a criminal.

Alban refused to answer the question but the Emperor continued his interrogation, demanding that he explain himself, renounce his new religious beliefs and as an act of atonement make sacrifices to the gods Apollo and Jupiter. In response to this demand, Alban replied that the gods worshipped by Severus were demons and 'deaf and dumb idols'. All those who foolishly worshipped them would go to Hell.

The Emperor by now was losing his patience and he commanded Alban, as a loyal citizen of the Empire, to make sacrifices to the gods. He promised that if he did this his official position would be restored without any stain on his record. Severus even promised to arrange a marriage for him with a woman of senatorial rank. However, the Emperor warned that if he failed to obey then his outspoken attack on the pagan religion and his imperial authority would not be tolerated. Again, Alban refused to sacrifice to the gods. He professed instead his spiritual allegiance to Christ. In desperation, Severus ordered him to be taken away and beaten until he agreed to obey the command. Despite this torture Alban was steadfast in his religious conviction and refused to make the sacrificial offerings required.

For the last time, Severus called for Alban to be brought before him. He told him plainly that either he made the sacrifices to the gods or he faced serious consequences. Alban declined and the Emperor ordered his execution for treason to the Roman state. As he was a Roman citizen this would be carried out by beheading. Alban was taken to an arena or amphitheatre next to a swiftly running stream (the River Ver). On the opposite bank a large crowd had gathered who had 'been summoned by divine prompting to attend the martyr'.

This crowd was so numerous that they took several hours to cross the bridge over the river and the execution was delayed. Because Alban and his military escort could not step on the bridge the saint prayed and the waters of the of the river parted. He and the soldiers could then walk across the dry river bed to his place of execution.

Swinson (1971) thinks that originally Alban was to be taken to the arena and thrown to wild animals or forced to fight to the death in an unfair gladiatorial combat. This was the normal way of dealing with convicted Christians during the persecutions. Swinson believes that because Alban was a Roman citizen it was decided to execute him by the sword outside the precincts of the Roman city. He cites the trials of Christians in Gaul in 177 where, on the orders of the Emperor, non-Romans were sentenced to the arena to be torn to pieces by wolves and bears while the Roman citizens were swiftly beheaded.

When Alban arrived at his place of death, the public executioner dropped his sword, threw himself at the saint's feet and asked Alban to pray for him. The soldiers escorting Alban fell back at this point and the saint was free to climb a nearby hill and address the crowd. He asked God to provide him with a drink of water as he was thirsty and a spring miraculously bubbled up out of the ground. The soldiers by now had arrested the subversive executioner and regained control of the situation. A second executioner was sent for and he finally carried out the sentence. The executioner who had refused to carry out his duty was beheaded alongside Alban. When the saint's head struck the ground his killer was instantly blinded by God.

Severus was so shocked by the events at the execution and the public support for Alban that he ordered the persecution of Christians to be halted. He said that the martyrdom of people like Alban only encouraged others and made the Christian religion prosper instead of hastening its abolition. In his introduction to Bede's A History of the English Church & People Leo Sherley-Price states that the miracles introduced into the story of Alban were 'pious forgeries' woven into an otherwise factual and historic account to impress the pagans with the superiority of the Christian saints over the Old Gods. Although Severus, apparently, abandoned his program against the Christians, those Emperors who followed him continued his work. In circa 250 Decius issued an edict designed to suppress Christian worship and in 257 Valerian prohibited Christian assemblies and confiscated the property of known followers of the new religion. In 286 Diolcetion became Emperor and during his reign ordered all Christian churches throughout the Empire to be destroyed and their congregations exterminated.

Christian sources claim many thousands of British Christians were massacred during this period, including the bishops of London, Llandaff, York, Carlisle and Caerleon. The persecution lasted from 303 to 306 but in 310 the Edict of Milan was passed granting religious freedom to Christians. This edict made it possible for Christianity to be practised in the Empire without fear of persecution or harassment. The Edict of Milan was the result of the tolerant attitude of the new British-born Emperor Constantine the Great, son of St Helen who was a British princess. He ruled from 306 until his death in 337 and achieved imperial office as a result of major internal conflicts and power struggles within the Empire. Constantine is said to have marched with his legions from Britain and seized the throne after a battle on the banks of the River Tiber. He was to become the most important figure after Jesus and Paul in the history of the Christian religion.

Constantine had been reared on the beliefs of the Sol Invicta cult promoted by a previous Emperor called Aurelian. This cultus practised sun worship and deified the Roman Emperor as the divine incarnation of the sun god. It was one of the first attempts in Roman culture to impose a monotheistic structure on religious practice, as opposed to the polytheistic worship practised by the average Roman citizen throughout the Empire. It had obvious parallels with Mithraism and also with early Christianity, where Jesus was sometimes referred to as 'the Sun of God' who illuminates the world.

There seems little reason to doubt Constantine was a practising pagan and remained so until his deathbed conversion to the new religion. For instance it was recorded that while fighting a military campaign in Gaul he experienced a vision of the sun god Apollo. However, in a subsequent campaign in 312 Constantine had a dream in which Jesus told him to put the Christian monogram Chi-Ro on the shields of his troops and they would win the battle next day. Another version of the legend says the Emperor had a vision on the eve of the battle and saw a blazing Christian cross in the sky. Underneath the cross, in letters of fire, were written the words In hoc signo vinces, or ' In this sign I conquer'.

When Constantine won the battle with a convincing victory and routed his enemies, he came to the conclusion that the Christian god must be a powerful deity and worthy of worship. The Emperor was a shrewd opportunist and the first in a long line of kings, statesmen, politicians and generals who would use Christianity to justify their actions. From this time on, while cunning enough not to openly profess a belief in Christianity so as to support the majority of his subjects, Constantine adopted a tolerant attitude to the religion and its followers.

During the rest of Constantine's reign paganism continued to be the prominent religious belief in the Empire and it flourished in an uneasy relationship with the minority Christian religion. Nobody at the time, however, could have been unaware of the imperial sympathy for the new religion. This period of tolerance allowed the Church to recover from the earlier persecutions, increase its numbers and attain more political power and influence within the administrational levels of the Empire's bureaucracy.

In 314 the Council of Arles was held in Gaul and this was one of the first of a series of such meetings of early Christian bishops and clergy to discuss and resolve the differences in belief and practice within Christianity at this time. It discussed such issues as whether Jesus had been the Son of God or merely an ordinary man. Those who disagreed with the decisions taken at these Councils were expelled from the early Church and outlawed as heretics, from the word heresy meaning 'to choose'.

Arles was attended by representatives of Christian churches from all parts of the Roman Empire, including North Africa, Spain, Italy, Germany, Gaul and, of course, Britain. This council was an important landmark in the history of early Christianity and the Church. It produced twenty two canons, or clerical decrees, on Christian attitudes to heresy, discipline, morality and the dating of Easter. This last decision was later to be of crucial importance in the power struggle between the Roman and Celtic Churches in Britain.

The presence of British representatives at Arles is an indication that at the beginning of the 4th century British Christianity was organised. The three British representatives are named as Eborius of York, Restitutus of

London and Adelphus or Adelfius of Lincoln. Whether they accepted the ruling at the Council on Easter is not known but this question was to become a serious controversy in the centuries to come. Representatives of the British Church also sent delegates to the subsequent Council of Nicea in 325, Sarica in 347 and Ariminum in 359.

It would appear by the 4th century Christianity was established in most of the large Romano-British towns in some sort of an organised form. Those in the military who were not Mithraists were Christians, as Constantine's vision of Jesus as a god of battle appealed to soldiers. Many wealthy Roman and Romano-British families were either openly Christian converts or sympathisers who practised in secret. The archaeological evidence suggests that in some family units both Christian and pagan worship was followed.

The form of Christianity followed at this time was called the Latin-Western tradition and, if the archaeological evidence can be believed, was strongly influenced by classical forms of paganism. Christian and pagan symbolism is often found together and the Romans adopted pre-Christian images, such as the dolphin and the centaur, to represent aspects of Christ or Christian mythology. Many of the social elite only practised the new religion for fashionable reasons and while paying lip service to Christian beliefs they still followed the worship of the Old Gods. This led to the early Church condemning those who attended Mass in the morning and gave offerings to lares, or household gods, in the afternoon. They condemned such practices saying 'the same mouth cannot utter the praises of Christ and Jupiter'. Unfortunately many people disagreed.

The pagan influence on early Christianity is illustrated by the fact that the first Romano-British churches were based on the architecture of the shrines to Mithras, Isis and other classical or Celtic deities. This may have been simply a matter of a lack of imagination resulting in the copying of existing designs for religious buildings. On the other hand it does offer a strong indication of the links between Christianity and paganism still existing at this period.

Archaeological evidence exists from the 4th century of Christians and pagans sharing the same building for worship. At Littlecote in Wiltshire a pagan shrine was excavated in a Roman villa dedicated to the god

Orpheus, who is depicted in the form of Apollo. Both these classical god forms were accepted by early Christians as saviour gods similar to Jesus. It has been put forward that this Orphic shrine may have been built by a nominally Christian family, as it combines both Christian and pagan symbolism. (Woodward 1992).

At Silchester an early Christian church had the same design as a Mithraic temple, while in 1963 a mosaic pavement was uncovered combining both pagan and Christian artwork. at Hinton St Mary in Dorset. It featured an illustration of Bellarophan spearing the Chimera and some historians believe this picture was copied by the Christian Church for their representation of St George slaying the dragon. The mosaic also showed the four evangelists in the form of the wind gods of the four quarters. In the centre of the mosaic was the clean shaven face of a dark-eyed young man who is probably Jesus. The earliest images of Jesus usually show him as clean shaven, dark and wearing his hair short in the Greek style. It is only later that the long haired, blue-eyed, bearded Anglo-Saxon image of Jesus began to dominates Christian iconography.

These finds provide evidence that both religious belief systems were practised equally and supported by people who were both Christians and pagans. In 314 two large churches were built at Canterbury and St Albans, but these seem to have been exceptions to the common practice. Archaeology offers a picture of Christian worship being carried out in small private chapels in houses and villas. With the brief reign of the pagan Emperor Julian (360-363) there was an increase in temple building in rural parts of Roman Britain. This temporarily halted the construction of new churches as people reverted back to the Old Ways.

Following Constantine's visionary experiences, the early Church realised they had a sympathiser at the highest level in the Empire and they took full advantage of this new and unique situation. They lost no time in naming Constantine as the 'beloved of God who guides and steers, in imitation of the Lord, all the affairs of the world'. The Church obviously saw the Emperor as the earthly representative of Christ, just as later the trappings of the Emperor would be projected on to the Pope. They even embraced the pagan symbolism of the imperial Sol Invicta cult and described Constantine as 'the light of the sun (who) illuminates those furthest from him with his rays.'

In return for this flattery and adoration, Constantine increased the power of the Church in the imperial power structure. He appointed Christians to key positions in the Roman administration, declared Sunday to be a public holiday (early Christians had observed Saturday as the Sabbath in the Jewish fashion but this was changed to Sunday or Sol's Day). The Emperor also granted the Church exemption from taxes and was responsible for exerting pressure on the pagan citizens of Rome by passing laws, at the Church's suggestion, outlawing the practice of the magical arts and divination.

Constantine's sympathetic approach to Christianity was continued after his death by his sons. However, the Church suffered a major, if short, setback when Julian became Emperor. He was a mystic intellectual and philosopher who wanted to restore the worship of the Old Gods. As a young man he had been initiated into Mysteries of the dark goddess Hecate, although outwardly he pretended to be a devout Christian during the reign of Constantine.

Julian sought to reverse the tide created by Constantine and restore the pagan religion because, even in these early days, he recognised the hypocrisy of the Church and the discrepancies between the Christian teachings and those who followed them. He was unhappy at the ease by which people living degenerate or evil lives could be so easily accepted into the Christian fold, providing they promised to repent and follow Jesus. Julian also objected to the gory images of Jesus hanging on the cross worshipped by the Christians. He regarded this image of death and suffering to be in contrast to the virile, pro-life, and often erotic, aspects of the old pagan religions. This view was also shared by some of the medieval Christian heretics who believed the image of the Risen Christ should be displayed in churches instead of the crucifixion scene.

Julian disliked Christianity for what he saw as valid reasons, however he was a tolerant man and provided the opportunity for all faiths, including the Christian one, to flourish throughout the Empire. He also shamelessly borrowed ideas from the Church, setting up pagan theological colleges, hospitals and orphanages that were exact copies of Christian ones. The colleges were set up to teach neophytes the principles of pagan religion and train them for the priesthood and were modelled on the early Christian monastic communities.

Julian's sudden and premature death in the Persian campaign brought a quick end to the pagan revival he had instigated. Julian' successor, Valentiniam, tolerated paganism but in 391 Emperor Theodosius banned all public pagan rituals and closed the temples in Rome. It had been rumoured that the person who stabbed Julian to death with a spear during the battle may not have been a Persian. In fact he was a disenchanted Christian centurion who objected to the Emperor's revival of pagan beliefs. Whether true or not, in the post-Julian era followers of the Old Religion faced increasing persecution from the authorities and the Church.

Around 315, or possibly in 335, one of the important figures in what later became known as 'Celtic Christianity' was born in Gaul. He was Martin of Tours who was later canonised by the Roman Church. St Martin was of pagan parentage and had briefly followed his father into the Roman Army. However as a teenager he had been converted to Christianity and he abandoned his military career for a life in the Church. He rose through the ranks and in 370 became the bishop of Tours.

As soon as he became bishop Martin began a crusade to convert the local peasantry. His method of conversion was to sweep through the countryside with a band of armed followers burning down the druid groves. Those who met the saint described him in unflattering terms as 'a despicable fellow quite unfit to be a bishop'. He had an insignificant appearance, was unkempt, badly dressed in dirty clothes and had 'disgraceful hair'. Personal hygiene was never a strong point with Christian monks and priests and throughout history cleanliness was regarded by the Church as ungodly and sinful. When the English martyr Thomas a' Beckett was killed, those who prepared the body for burial noticed his robe was rotting and infested with lice. They regarded this as a sure sign that he had been a very saintly and holy man.

Martin lived with eighty monks and priests at a community just outside Tours. The bishop lived in a wooden shelter while the others inhabited living quarters hollowed out from cliffs on the banks of the River Loire. Martin is significant in the early history of the Celtic Church because he introduced the monastic tradition into southern Europe from the Middle East. It was this tradition that was to provide the socio-cultural and organisational framework for the early Celtic Church in Gaul, Britain and Ireland. Martin also baptised Elen, or Helen, the wife of Magnus

Maximus (aka Macsen Wledig). He was the last Roman governor of Wales and his wife was largely responsible for establishing Celtic Christianity in Britain in the 5th century.

Elen was the daughter of King Octavius of the Gewissei tribe of South Wales, while Maximus was a Roman senator of Hispanic origin born in Galecia in Spain. In one version of his life he came to Britain in 368 as an official with Theodosius the Great and attained the rank of Commander of the Western Fleet. Shortly after this elevation he was appointed governor of the Welsh province of Roman Britain.

In *The Mabinogion*, the collection of Welsh legends and myths compiled in the last century by Lady Charlotte Guest from various medieval manuscripts, there is a story that Maximus was drawn to Britain by dreaming about Elen and then by an offer from Octavius of her hand in marriage. As Octavius was supposed to have been one of the high kings of Britain, if not the King of Britain, this was an offer the ambitious Roman general could not refuse. It is said that Elen ordered a major construction of roads across Britain (or possibly just Wales) linking the Roman forts. These highways were called 'the roads of Elen of the Hosts', because of the large number of men employed on their construction and the story that they would not have done the work for anyone else but the Welsh princess.

This strange legend has naturally promoted considerable speculation as to the nature of these roads. Some Earth Mysteries researchers have attempted to link them with ley lines or landscape alignments. In his book The Old Straight Track (Methuen 1925), Alfred Watkins, the grandfather of modern Earth Mysteries, claims that Elen was the daughter of Constantius, the Duke of Colchester. He was the 'Old King Cole' of the famous nursery rhyme who marched his men up to the top of the hill and down again. He links the name Cole or Coel with ley lines, druids, omens, wizards, diviners and magical alphabets.

Elen is often confused with Constantius' wife Helen or Helena who, as we saw earlier, was the mother of Emperor Constantine the Great and died in 330. Elen also had a son called Constantine and is often confused with the earlier Emperor. Interestingly, just to confuse matters further, Maximus is said to be descended from Helena's family. This supposed link between

Elen and ley lines has led to fanciful speculation that she was really a Celtic goddess who was transformed into a saint.

In 383 the Roman Empire was plunged into political chaos by its division between three rulers. The Roman legions in Britain declared Maximus as Emperor and after campaigning in Gaul he marched on Rome in 387 to claim the imperial throne. In 388 he was defeated in battle by Theodsius, captured and beheaded. While in Gaul Maximus held his court at Treves and it was during this period he and Elen met Martin of Tours.

Maximus does not seem to have liked Christians very much and, despite his friendship with Martin, even persecuted them. Elen seems to have embraced the new religion as did many of her followers. The 9th century Historia Brittanum says Brittany was settled by the British (Welsh) troops who had sailed with Maximus and Elen across the Channel.

After the death of her husband, Elen returned to Wales and it is claimed became the supreme ruler of the 'West of Britain'. This included Wales, Anglesey and the Isle of Man. She took over the major Roman fortresses at Dinas Emrys in Snowdonia, Carmarthen in Dyfed and Caerleon on the Welsh border. These were all Celtic sacred centres and the roads she built to link them became known as Sarn Elen or Elen's Way. During her lifetime she established several Christian settlements in Wales and after her death her son, Constantine, continued her work. He is credited with importing the monastic tradition taught by St Martin into Wales and forming the ground structure of the Celtic Church.

Chapter Three
The Celtic Church

The end of the Roman presence in Britain came in the first decade of the 5th century, as the Roman legions responsible for the country's external defence gradually withdrew to defend Rome itself against attacks from the Goths, Huns and Vandals. The decision by the governor of Wales to leave for Gaul had left the legions in southern Britain seriously undermanned. Maximus had appointed one of his trusted officers as regent but his rule was unpopular and eventually he was assassinated. With the Roman army weakened and poorly led the country was open to invasion from the Picts in the north and the Irish Gaels from the west.

The retreat of the legions from Wales in particular was to begin a 500 year period of internal wars between rival princes, invasions by Saxons, Picts, Gaels and Vikings and outbreaks of famine and plague. Generally law and order broke down and anarchy and chaos ruled as the Roman exodus left a power vacuum.

As a result of this instability many Welsh Celts fled the country and they joined with the remnants of Maximus' British troops to form the new Celtic nation of Armorica or Brittany. Several of the Celtic Christian missionaries who later travelled to Wales and Cornwall in the 5th century and became saints were Bretons of Welsh descent. Brittany also had an important role to play in the medieval revival of the Arthurian legends and the creation of the Grail romances, as we shall discover later.

In the last days of the Roman occupation a few Saxon mercenaries had arrived in Britain to help the army repel the raids by the Picts and Irish. Saxon pirates had also made their own raids on southern Britain and in 367 they had joined forces with the Pictish tribes to over-run Hadrian's Wall. In 408 a large number of Saxon mercenaries were invited to Britain to help the Romano-British nobles seize power from the retreating and demoralised Roman legions.

In 410 the new leaders of Britain were even forced to ask the Emperor for help against the foreign raiders. A limited number of Roman troops did return in 412, but by 418 all the legions had returned to Rome. At the end of the 420s the Romano-Celtic leader Vortigern, the 'High King' who had previously been king of the Celtic tribes in South Wales, in some desperation invited the Saxon warriors Horsa and Hengist to become mercenaries in his service. This, in hindsight, was a fatal mistake on his part.

When Vortigern eventually thanked them for their help and asked them to leave the Saxon warlords refused. In fact they not only refused to go but they turned on their former masters, demanding land in exchange for the help they had given. A Celto-Saxon war broke out and at first the British managed to hold their own. Then Horsa and Hengist called a 'peace conference' and invited all the leaders of the Celtic tribes to attend. This was a trap and the British leaders were massacred leading to a Saxon victory.

It is claimed that Vortigern was a Christian king who was excommunicated by the bishop of London for incest with his daughter. Following this he converted to the Pelagian heresy and, allegedly, had invited the Saxons to Britain to support his rule over its Christian people. It is further claimed that Vortigern gave up his heretical views and adopted the pagan ways of his wife, Rowena, who was the daughter of Hengist (Morgan 1938). Reading this story one is reminded of the famous account of Vortigern at Dinas Emrys in North Wales consulting wizards about the building of a tower and the vision of two dragons seen in a pool by the boy-seer Ambrosius.

When I lived at Harrow-on-the-Hill as a child there was a strange, garbled legend about Horsa and Hengist connecting them with Horsendon Hill at nearby Perivale. It was said that Horsa was buried under the hill and the ghosts of he and his warriors rode out from it on certain nights. This legend also said that his wife (sic) Rowena used to dance with the faeries at nearby Perivale, the 'Vale of the Faeries'. Like all good pagans she renounced her wicked ways and became the abbess of a convent in Ealing.

In Saxon times Harrow-on-the Hill was an important sacred centre and its name means 'sanctuary on the hill'.

British resistance to the Saxons, Angles and Jutes was allegedly led at this time by the Roman-British chieftain and warlord Arthur and his warriors, later the knights of the Round Table. He is supposed to have been killed in battle around 470 or possibly at the beginning of the 5th century, other sources place him firmly in the latter century and is associated with many of the Celtic saints of the period. Whatever the truth of the matter by the end of the 5th century most of southern and eastern England, as it was now known, was under Saxon control and they were pushing northwards and westwards to consolidate their position.

Meanwhile in Wales, an Irish tribe known as the Deisi had invaded the south-west of the country and had united with the surviving remnants of the Celtic Demetae people to form a new kingdom. In North Wales the resident Irish Gaels were ousted at the beginning of the 5th century by a Celtic king from the north called Cunneda. He, in turn, had been driven south from Strathclyde by the marauding Picts.

It is against this confused, anarchic and bloody backdrop that the so-called 'Age of the Celtic Saints' began. It also saw the development of the Celtic Church in Wales, north-west England and the Scottish Border, Cornwall and Ireland as a cohesive entity and a powerful missionary force. The missionaries from Ireland and Brittany who arrived in Britain established a distinctive form of Christian religion now known to history as 'Celtic Christianity'. They in turn were joined by or taught native-born Christians who ran their own missions and centres for Christian teaching and worship. This was a not an isolated development in history, as some may think, for the Celtic Church regarded itself as a direct descendant from the Glastonbury community of the 1st century and it also retained links with the Gallic Church and, to a lesser extent, with Rome.

Many of the druids who had survived the Roman occupation seem to have been fairly easily converted to the new religion. In some cases, as is often the way with new recruits, they became its most zealous followers and led the missions to convert those who followed the Old Ways. In ancient times every king had his druid or shaman who acted as a counsellor and advisor on state matters, in addition to his usual role as celebrant of the religious rites of the tribe. When these kings converted Christian priests, some of whom had been druids, took over this important role.

The tales of the Celtic saints, as related by their hagiographers, describe them battling with unconverted druids, Saxon priests and 'wise women' (priestesses) and the demons (pagan gods) they worshipped. In these popular stories the saints often fight fire with fire and use miraculous powers any pagan priest would envy. Many of the saints are depicted as wonder-workers and there is often very little to distinguish their alleged supernatural powers from the magical arts employed by those they were trying to convert.

As in Roman times, the Celtic version of Christianity was at first the religion of the ruling classes in society. It was only later that it was imposed downwards on the pagans or pagani, the country folk who still worshipped the Old Gods. The Welsh princes, for instance, were converted, or decided to pay lip-service to, Christianity after an initial struggle. Many of the most famous of the Celtic saints were also of royal blood or belonged to the old Romano-British aristocracy. The rulers patronised the missionaries and this increased their power and influence within the social structure of post-Roman Britain. According to the Welsh Triads, the family of Cunneda in North Wales were the first royal house to grant land and privileges to 'the saints of the Isle of Britain.'

The pagan influence on the cult of the saints, and the deliberate siting of Christian settlements near pagan temples and shrines, is a significant factor in the early history of Celtic Christianity. At first the early Christians and the pagans appear to have co-existed in a situation resembling mutual tolerance, even if it was tinged with suspicion on both sides. As the Celtic Church grew in size and corresponding political power the balance shifted. The Age of the Celtic Saints in the 5th and 6th centuries is marked by increasing conflict between the new faith and the Old Religion. It is characterised by a struggle for spiritual supremacy between the missionaries and the pagan tribal chieftains and druids. Earlier claims that Britain was a country where Christianity was well established are not borne out by the struggle for power between the missionaries and their pagan opponents in the Celtic fringes of the British Isles.

The earliest of the Celtic Christian sites in western Britain that can be identified as such by archaeological research are associated with the burial grounds used for new converts to the faith. These appeared first in the 5th century and were in the form of small cemeteries surrounded by a circular or oval earthwork in the pre-Christian style, or a stone wall of crude design. Often these early cemeteries were placed near to pagan sanctuaries and burial places that were either still used or had been abandoned.

This policy was an indication of the religious divisions, and the sense of religious continuity, at this period. Some people would have been pagan while others had embraced the new religion. While this situation of dual faith continued, and was tolerated by the embryonic Celtic Church because they had little choice at this time, the dead would have been buried by Christian or pagan rites in their own exclusive cemeteries. It was also Christian policy to take over pagan cemeteries for their own burials. These early burial places may have been used exclusively by local Christian families or groups or by communities of monks and missionaries living in the area.

The tribal kings and chieftains often owned a special epic of land known as a llan or 'enclosure'. These were usually described as ' clear open spaces' and were defined by a surrounding earthwork or henge. With the coming of Christianity and the conversion of many of these tribal rulers, the llan was often given to the priest. They became the site of the early mud-and-wattle, thatched roofed churches and in the 12th century many of these were rebuilt by the Normans as stone buildings.

Many Welsh churches, especially in West Wales, have circular or oval churchyards and are situated on or near earthworks of Iron Age or prehistoric origin. A classic example is at Eglwys Cymyn, near Laugharne in Carmarthenshire (Dyfed). Here there is a circular churchyard with a church built on top of an ancient earth mound. As a place of Christian worship it dates from the 5th century and before that it was probably a pagan temple or sanctuary. A prehistoric standing stone is stored in an oak chest in the vestry and it is reputed to have belonged to stone circle that once stood on the mound.

The name Elglwys Cymyn, or the church of Cymyn, derives from a mistranslation of the Latin Cunegi. This is the name found inscribed on the standing stone in the Ogham script imported into West Wales by the Irish in the 4th and 5th centuries. This stone was only found in 1880, when it was being used as a step on the church path. St Cunegi or Cunignus was a Celtic missionary and the prehistoric stone was dedicated as a monument to his daughter, Anna.

The church was rededicated to St Margaret of Antioch by Sir Guy de Bryan, the Norman lord of the manor at Laugharne from 1350 to 1391. The stained glass windows, dating only from around 1900, contain some very interesting symbolism, possibly inspired or influenced unconsciously by its ancient origins. The east window depicts St Margaret spearing a dragon, described by the church guide book as 'a symbol of evil'. Joan of Arc can be seen in lower panel of the window receiving spirit messages from SS Margaret, Catherine and Michael. The central light shows St Margaret of Scotland holding the sceptre of her great-uncle, Edward the Confessor. In this illustration the Holy Spirit in the form of a white dove descends, Gnostic fashion, on to Jesus hanging on the cross.

The south window has St Michael killing Lucifer (the `light bearer' and a god of light before he became the Christian Devil) in the form of another dragon. In the early Middle Ages many of the ancient churches in Wales, the West Country and Cornwall were rededicated to this saint/archangel. As the guardian of the gates of Hell in Christian mythology Michael was regarded as a suitable patron for churches built on the old pagan sites and a suitable opponent for the pagan powers of darkness still believed to haunt their locality.

The all important motif of the dragon is featured once more at this former pagan site in another window depicting St George. Although he was of Greek origin he was adopted by crusaders and became the patron saint of England. Some folklorists have identified him as a Christian version of the Celtic god Bel or Belinus. Another window in the church features St Nicholas, patron saint of children, who is better known as Santa Claus. Originally Santa was the Norse god Odin, who rode the night sky as the leader of the Wild Hunt, as did Gwyn ap Nudd at Glastonbury.

Unconscious pagan symbolism can also be found at the church of St Lawrence at Marros not far up the coast from Laugherne. Outside the 13th century church is a very unusual war memorial in the form of a Megalithic trilithon, similar to the ones at Stonehenge. Local people, if asked, will tell tourists, rather unconvincingly. it actually represents a coffin carried by two bearers. Marros church stands on a pre-Christian site and in 1868 several large pottery vessels dating from the Bronze Age and containing ashes and bones were dug up in the church grounds. This is probably the remains of a cemetery but more speculative theories hint at a pagan sanctuary or druidic grove and human sacrifices.

At Llansadwrnen, two miles east of Laugharne, there is a circular churchyard offering proof the church was built on a site of pagan worship. This is confirmed by a large standing stone secreted in a broom cupboard on the left of the porch and directly under the tower. This is a lone survivor of many standing stones that used to be in the vicinity of the church, probably belonging to a stone circle or a row of stones in alignment. When i visited the church some years ago the local farmer next to the church told me he had uprooted some of the standing stones because "They got in the way". Unfortunately he could not remember where he had dumped there or if he did felt reluctant to tell an 'incomer' like me.

About half a mile north of the village is Holy Stone Corner. This takes its name from a pile of stones in a field surrounded by a walled enclosure. Local tradition says in the old days coffin bearers on the way to funerals used to rest the corpse on the stones while they had their refreshments. As these stones are some distance from the road, and are possibly of prehistoric origin, this story seems a little unlikely. On the other hand the stones may indicate the route of one of the ancient 'death roads', or spirit paths, connecting the church with other, now long lost, pagan sites in the area.

At Yspty Cynfyn, near the evocatively named Devil's Bridge on the A4120 road ten miles from Aberystwyth, standing stones from a former stone circle can still be seen embedded in the churchyard wall The church is dedicated to St John, who is a significant figure in Celtic Christian tradition, and the original church on the site is believed to have dated from the 5th century. Outside the church door stands an ancient yew reputed, like those at the pagan/Christian site of Nevern in Pembrokeshire (Dyfed), to 'bleed' at the full moon.

A footpath, reopened. by Dyfed County Council in 1988, passes alongside the churchyard wall and then drops down into a wooded gorge. A bridge then spans the Afon Rheidol and on the other side of the river the path leads uphill through a conifer plantation on to open hilly moor land where a small stone circle can be found. Local tradition says the Order of Knight Templars owned the land around Yspty Cynfyn and this was inherited by the Knight Hospitalers, or Knights of St John, when the Order was suppressed for heresy in the early 14th century. Hence the first part of the church's Welsh name meaning 'hospital'.

Legends also associate Yspty Cynfyn with the Holy Grail allegedly brought by Joseph of Arimathea from the Holy Land in the 1st century. This version of the legend says that when Joseph died the safekeeping of the Grail was entrusted to his disciples and eventually the holy relic passed into the care of the monks of Glastonbury Abbey.

When the abbey was closed by the orders of Henry VIII, and the abbot was executed on the Tor, a small group of monks fled to West Wales carrying the Grail. For a time they were given sanctuary at Strata Florida Abbey, where the Grail became the focus of a healing cult. When this hiding place became unsafe the monks left and finally sought refuge at the house of Nant Eos, a few miles from Yspty Cynfyn. There they were given sanctuary by the Powell family.

When the last of the monks died it was said the guardianship of the Grail passed to the family and he told them with his dying breath to keep it safe until such time as the Church was worthy enough to reclaim it. A small cup of olive wood alleged to be the Grail, or at least a copy of it, was used for healing at Nant Eos until the beginning of this century. People travelled from miles around to drink from the cup in the hope of a cure for their ailments.

The Powell family finally moved from Nant Eos in the 1950s and at that time it is understood the healing vessel was deposited in a bank vault in Hertfordshire. A few years ago when I visited Nant Eos this large country house was empty and in a poor state of repair, with crumbling stonework and broken, or boarded up, windows. It seemed to me that the glory surrounding the Grail, if that is what it was, had departed with it and left a wasteland in its place.

Many other churches in West Wales have standing stones within their precincts, including St David's church at Bridell on the Cardigan to Tenby road, but perhaps the most famous example in the area is at Nevern, off the Cardigan to Fishguard road, which was mentioned earlier. The church is cruciform in plan and dedicated to the Irish saint, Brynach. The present church dates from the 14th century, has a Norman tower and was extensively restored in Victorian times. It stands in the shadow of an Iron Age hill fort that had a motte-and-bailey castle built on it in medieval times. The stone ruins of this can still be seen in the undergrowth on top of the mound and there are trees growing out of the walls. The mound has a peculiar atmosphere at times and there is a dragon legend associated with it.

This hill fort was occupied in pre-Christian times by a Celtic chief called Clether and his llan became the site of the original church. The enclosure was bounded by a brook called the Caman and the church guide book suggests its waters were used for both sacred and secular purposes. The district later came under the control of Maelgwyn Gwynedd, who died of the plague in 547, and he made further donations of land to the church in his lifetime.

In the churchyard stands a 10th century Celtic cross, decorated with Celtic and Scandinavian pagan and Christian symbols. Just outside the porch is a standing stone carved with an inscription in Ogham and Latin. The church guide says it dates from the 5th century, which it probably does in its inscribed form, but there can be little doubt it is far older. The churchyard also contains the grave of the Rev. John Jones, whose bardic name was Tegid. He was the vicar at Nevern from 1842 to 1852 and helped Lady Charlotte Guest translate the old medieval tales of The Mabinogion into English for her famous edition.

Growing in the churchyard is a magnificent avenue of ancient yews, the symbol of death, eternal life and rebirth. At times a dark red resin flows from the trunks of these trees. It resembles menstrual blood and for that reason in recent years Nevern has become a place of pilgrimage for pagan feminists, who regard it, rightly or wrongly, as a site dedicated to the Dark Goddess.

Inside the church are two other standing stones, now embedded in concrete in the window sills They were discovered as late as 1906 hidden in the walls of the so-called 'priest's chamber' over the chapel. These chambers are a common feature in old Welsh churches. They were used by the priest, or guardian of the church, either as a private chapel or even as living space. These stone were regarded as an important discovery as they are extensively inscribed in both Latin and Ogham. They provided the Celtic 'Rosetta Stone' for linguists to decipher and translate the Ogham alphabet. Near to these stones is a slab in the wall carved with an unusual, rather 'feminine', version of a Celtic elongated cross. It has two 'cords' growing out of a single column and then interlacing to form the shape of a cross and is surmounted by the usual Celtic knot design. With a little imagination, it does resemble a human female form and has been seized upon as further evidence this site is connected with Goddess worship.

Yew trees can also be found in abundance at the church site at Meidrim, near Carmarthen. Here the church was built on top of a large mound of prehistoric origin and is surrounded by a tell-tale circular churchyard. The boundary of the mound is also marked by over thirty ancient yew trees guarding the church. Another church with a pagan and Celtic Christian history is at Glasgwn in Radnorshire (Powys) and it is dedicated to St David. Local folklore says the church was actually founded by the saint. There is certainly evidence of an earlier monastic settlement built before the medieval church. The present building, as at Meidrim, was erected on a mound, believed to have been a Bronze Age burial place. A semi-circle of yews surrounds the west and south-west of the church and it stands in a circular churchyard.

Also in Radnorshire, a few miles from the previous site, is the church of St Michael at Llanfihangel Nant Melan. Again there is evidence of a Celtic church built on a pagan shrine. It used to have a circle of yew trees and there are many ancient burial mounds in the area. The church is dedicated to St Michael because there is a legend of a dragon that used to roam the nearby Radnor Forest. This could be a folk memory of the arrival of the missionaries and their battle with the local pagans.

The old pagan shrines were sometimes renamed after Celtic saints. At Maentwrog church in Gwynedd a standing stone, once part of a stone circle, can be seen in the graveyard next to the church wall. It is in the vicinity of more yew trees and is named after a local missionary called St Twrog who died around 610. After his death it is said the locals built a chapel in his name inside the stone circle.

Cromlechs, or prehistoric burial chambers, in Wales were often called Yr Hen Eglwys or the Old Church. This was because of local traditions concerning druids who were converted and then used the old sites for worship and preaching. At Llanhamlach in Breconshire (Powys) there are the remains of a small cromlech under a yew tree and surrounded by stones. This is known locally as Ty Illytd or Illtyd's House and is named after the famous Celtic saint. Nearby are stones carved with Christian crosses and a standing stone called Maen Illtyd. Some people say the cromlech was actually utilised by St Illtyd as a hermit's cell. This reminds us of the pre-Christian use of burial mounds as places for initiation and visionary vigils. One of the most famous of these in Wales is Pentre Ifan in the Nevern Valley which is known locally as 'The Womb of Cerridwen'. In Celtic times local folklore says a druidic college used to flourish nearby and Pentre Ifan was used for their initiation ceremonies.

West of Brecon, in the parish of Delynnog, is the church of Llaniltud (the llan of Illtyd) and near to its a Megalithic monument where medieval villagers gathered on the eve of the saint's festival to hold an all night vigil. This monument consisted of two large standing stones placed at each end of a small tumulus next to a pool. Although this site is obviously pre-Christian, local people insisted it was the grave of the saint. The fact they gathered here on the eve of his festival is a clue this was originally some kind of pagan observance, possibly honouring the dead. The Celts celebrated their seasonal festivals on the evening before the actual date as they followed a lunar based calendar.

Outside Abercastle on the north Pembrokeshire coast between Fishguard and St David's is another small cromlech, situated in a beautiful setting overlooking the sea. It is known as Carreg Samson or 'stones of Samson' and is named after the Breton saint. The frequent and continued association of Celtic saints with these important prehistoric sites offers yet another powerful indicator of the way Christian and pagan beliefs intermingled during the 5th century. This tradition continued into early medieval times and still survives in the local memory and folklore today.

Many of the Celtic crosses found scattered across Wales date from the early medieval period but some were originally standing stones converted into Christian monuments. At Carren in North Wales a standing stone can be seen in the churchyard wall. This, and the shaft of the ancient churchyard cross, may be part of a former burial chamber on the site. the capstone of this burial chamber bears cup-and-ring marks and now forms the base of the cross. These Celtic crosses and inscribed stones associated with the saints and early Christian settlements were widely venerated and treated as sacred objects with healing and miraculous powers. This belief survived in Wales until at least the 12th century when Giraldus Cambrensis remarked upon it (Redknap 1991). Such ancient beliefs again provided ample proof of a survival of pre-Christian ideas relating to the sacred stones worshipped in pagan times by the Celts and earlier peoples.

To Celtic Christians not only was the actual church building sacred, and a place where the ancient right of sanctuary applied, but this sacredness extended to the boundaries of the (often circular) churchyard. This belief is a relic of the stone circles and ritual earthworks used for religious purposes in the pre-Celtic period. Sometimes former pagan burial grounds were incorporated into churchyards as the earlier sacred sites were taken over.

One Welsh example is at Warren in south Pembrokeshire, where a large prehistoric tumulus used to stand in a field known as Churchways, about half a mile from the church itself. In 1800 the mound was excavated and revealed numerous human skeletons, animal bones, pottery and stones carved with symbols. These included an equal-armed cross in a circle, later familiar as the principal symbol of the Celtic Church. Also discovered near the tumulus were the walls of an ancient chapel. Local folklore informs us this was the remains of a church built by early Christians who came to the area. It was pulled down by 'the other people' because it was too close to where they buried their dead.

Gregory (1991) says that while there are records of two Roman soldiers being martyred as Christians at Caerleon on the Welsh Border during

Diocletion's persecution, there are no records of any churches being built in Wales during the Roman period. He does however cite considerable evidence to suggest Roman settlements, and possibly temples, were take over in the 5th century as sites for Celtic Christian churches. One of these sites is at Caernarfon, where the parish churchyard at Llanbeblig boasts a Roman altar.

Sacred springs of pre-Christian origin were also closely connected with the 5th century cult of the Celtic saints and were taken over as holy wells. Jones (1950) lists a total of 1179 wells and of these 437 have associations with Celtic saints and 369 had healing properties. People patronised these wells not only because of their remarkable healing powers but also used them for divination and folk rituals to bring luck and good fortune.

Special rituals were carried out at the wells containing elements of the old Celtic and pre-Celtic water worship. These rites included walking around the well three times, drinking its water from a human skull and chanting prayers. Copying the practice in pagan times of making sacrificial offerings to the water deities at sacred springs and pools, visitors threw bent pins, brass buckles, coins and flowers into these wells. Candles were burnt and rag offerings hung in the branches of trees nearby. After drinking the healing water the patient had to sleep on a stone near the well for the cure to be successful. In Gwynedd one of these stones was known as Carreg Y Delefod or the Stone of the Rite.

The take-over of pagan sites by Christianity and the adaptation of pagan forms of worship to suit the requirements of the new religion, or as a continuing folk tradition, was not of course unique to Wales. The examples I have given above have been used because most of the sites mentioned are familiar to me. All over Britain in the Roman and Saxon periods ancient religious sites were replaced by Christian churches and monasteries and it has been said that the majority of pre-Reformation churches stand on former pagan sites.

The earliest Welsh churches, as elsewhere, were of a simple design and construction. In fact most were similar to secular buildings used for everyday living. Archaeological evidence reveals small chapels built of wood with a thatched roof. The floors would have been of earth and were strewn with rushes to keep them clean and dry. In the 5th and 6th centuries the erection of stone buildings was unusual, but not unknown. Examples survive of so-called beehive cells (named from their shape) used by the monks and hermits in this period. (Woodward 1992).

Where substantial church buildings were built using stone they were usually copies of the early churches erected by Christian converts in Roman times. Excavations at Silchester in 1892 unearthed the remains of one of these early churches and it gives us some idea of the ground plan and design of the Celtic Christian churches in Wales and elsewhere. It was oriented east to west, with a central part measuring thirty feet by ten, with an apex in the west end. Aisles five feet wide extended on either side and there was seven foot porch. The nave had a red tile floor while in the apse was a smaller section, about five feet square, of more elaborate paving. This paved area (the altar site?) is a Roman feature, possibly borrowed from pagan temples, and is not likely to have featured in post-Roman Celtic churches.

In south-west England, which came under Celtic Christian influence when Welsh and Breton missionaries arrived, it has been suggested many Romano-British temples were converted for Christian use or replaced by churches. In one example a statue of the Roman god Mercury was broken up and deliberately buried in the foundations (Woodward 1992). In the 7th century in southern England other Romano-British temples, and Saxon sanctuaries, were taken over and converted into Roman Catholic churches. This process would have continued into the 8th and 9th centuries when many of these former temples were destroyed and new churches built on the sites.

There are references to ecclesia rotundae or round churches in 6th century Wales. This unusual shape is a strong sign of pagan influence and because of the obvious association with the Old Religion the idea of building churches in this form was discouraged. It briefly experienced a revival in the 12th to 14th centuries when the heretical Templars, who were active at that time in Cardiganshire and Pembrokeshire, built round churches and chapels. The most famous of these is the Temple in the law courts off Fleet Street in London. When the Order was suppressed by the Church the building of round churches fell out of favour and has only recently been revived.

The theological beginnings of the Celtic Church were influenced by the Middle Eastern ascetics or desert hermits and by the monastic tradition. Early Christian monks followed the extreme example of St Anthony, who is credited with inventing the monastic life in the 4th century, and hermits sought solitude in the nearest wilderness where they believed they would become closer to God. They lived in caves or crude shelters and devoted themselves to a solitary life of meditation, prayer and inner contemplation. They claimed this austere lifestyle gave them a mystical insight into the mysteries of nature, the universe and divinity.

It was not an original concept, very little in Christianity was, and in earlier times the shaman or priest of the tribe was often a loner or even a social outcast. He or she would leave the tribal community to spend long periods of time in the forest seeking spiritual awareness and enlightenment. They communed with the spirit world, the ancestral dead, their totem animals and the Old Gods. This mixture of shamanic paganism and early Christian mysticism came together in the cult of the Celtic Christian saints. It manifested as in the love of nature, sometimes bordering on pantheism, found in the stories of saints living in the primeval wildwood with only birds and animals as companions.

It is now known, from the recent archaeological dig at Tintagel in north Cornwall, that the old sea routes that brought the Phoenicians here, were still in use during the Age of the Saints. There was a widespread trade between the Mediterranean area and Britain at this time. Wine, for instance, was being imported from as far away as Rhodes, Cyprus and the Greek islands for use in the Celtic Christian eucharist. This trading exchange would have naturally included ideas and spiritual concepts as well as people and material goods. It has been suggested the Celtic Church may have been influenced by Coptic Christian ideas from Egypt at this period. (Toulson 1987)

As we have seen Elen and her son Constantine are credited with introducing the monastic tradition into Britain in the 5th century. It is known the first Irish monasteries appeared around that time, but they these early monastic centres were very different from the medieval ones established under the Roman Church. They were based on a communal family unit, with the wives and children of the married clergy taking an active role. The monks choosing to lead a celibate life by choice .

Celibacy for the Welsh and English clergy was not strictly enforced until the 12th century. Then the Synod of London in 1103 declared it was forbidden for any new priests entering holy orders to be married.

In the Celtic monastic centres the senior clergy took the role of teachers, administrators and priests. Others in the household were cooks, gardeners, embroiders (of vestments and altar cloths etc), masons, carpenters, smiths, jewellers and farmers. The monastery was in essence a self-contained, self -sufficient microcosm of society outside. They were built up of small groups of huts or cells surrounded by a stone wall and often enclosed in a henge or earthwork. They were often located near the coast to protect them from attacks from the land. When the Saxons and Vikings invaded these sea-facing sites were a distinct disadvantage.

Conditions inside the monasteries were extremely austere. The monks '...slept on beds of skins, used stone pillows covered with bracken and their only furniture consisted of a wooden bench, a rush lamp and a cross.' (Toulson 1987) The monks wore animal skin clothing and added furs in the winter. The life for permanent residents of the Celtic monasteries consisted of an endless cycle of hard manual labour and prayer.

The missionary efforts conducted by the early Celtic Church were centred on small groups of monks sent out from these centres by the abbot or bishop. Their mission was to travel in specific areas preaching and converting. They would settle in their chosen location, attach themselves to a particular tribe and live a simple life based on the monastic rule of their parent religious house. The early organisational development of the Church was therefore along 'tribal' lines, rather then being based on a diocese administering a particular region or group of churches.

A group of these missionary-monks was known in Welsh as a cor or choir, from the druidic world for a circle. It is possibly related to the Greek khonos, or chorus, in the sense of a group of people singing or speaking together. The monks parent house was known as a Bangor from Ban, meaning high, chief or principle, and gor, a variant of cor. Ban-gor literally means 'high circle' and refers to the ruling body controlling the cori or circles.

The early Celtic Church in Wales was divided into three main groupings or classes. These were the holy men, such as Illytd and Cadoc who were responsible for founding the original monastic centres and teaching colleges; the bishops, who were the early saints like Dewi (David) and Teilo; and the hermits, who were groups of wandering saints or 'pilgrim saints'. They travelled across the land and sea between Wales, Cornwall and Brittany converting the pagans by example.

Female saints seem to have been included in the last category although there were also women abbots and, if legend can be believed, female bishops in the Celtic Christian persuasion In practice all these separate categories became blurred and you find all the saints taking the roles described at different times

The holy men were probably the most important category because in a sense they were the 'founding fathers' of the Celtic Church and its monastic organisation. The bishops carried on their work, administering and organising the missionary work. The hermits or 'pilgrim saints' were the mystics of Celtic Christianity. Their solitary lives of prayer, devotion and meditation., combined with the influence of pagan Celtic spirituality, created the nature mysticism often associated with the cult of the Celtic saints and the later Grail legends.

This pattern of Celtic Christian settlement and organisation survived until after the creation of the four bishoprics in Wales. These were at Bangor in Gwynedd, North Wales; St Asaph in Powys, Mid-Wales, St David's in West Wales and Llandaff in Gwent, South Wales. While this centralisation of power created a more organised hierarchical structure to the Church, it seems unlikely that the method of local organisation and missionary work changed very much for many years.

Each of the new centres were independent and consisted of a monastery, school and college under the control of a bishop. Other monasteries in each area presided over by independent abbots gradually relinquished their power to these new centres of authority founded by the saints. By the end of the 6th century the major monasteries were established, either under saintly or royal patronage. The number of monks who occupied these sites seem to have been enormous, if we can believe the later accounts. For instance, Bede claims Bangor Iscoed had over two thousand monks, while Caer Emrys and Bangor Wydrin (Glastonbury) boasted two thousand four hundred monks each. This gives a grand total of over nine thousand monks at these sites alone.

It is always possible that Bede, writing several centuries later, was correct or it is possible that he, and other biased clerical historians, exaggerated or even invented these high figures to misrepresent the Celtic Church as more powerful in pagan areas then it actually was at this time. These large groups were allegedly divided into smaller groupings of one hundred monks and they took shifts throughout the night and day reciting continuous prayers. Considering the population at this time, it is almost certain the figures quoted above in fact had little relationship to the strength of the Celtic Church at this period in its history. .

Chapter Four
The Age of the Saints

The period covered by the 5th and 6th centuries, and especially the time-span from 450 to 589, is popularly known in Church history as 'The Age of the Celtic Saints'. The period immediately preceding it saw the withdrawal of the Roman legions and the invasions by the Picts, Irish and Saxons. It also saw the greatest threat posed to the early Church in Britain since the Roman persecutions, the Pelagian heresy. This alternative version of Christianity originated with Morgan, the Abbot of Bangor, who was also known as Pelagius. It is possible he may have been one of the famous 'Christian druids' who had converted from the Old Faith and then attempted to remould Christianity to suit his beliefs. Between 400 and 450 the heresy spread like wildfire through the British Isles and into Europe. As late as the middle of the 6th century St David was fighting the heresy in Wales and it also appeared again in northern Britain in the 7th century.

The Pelagian heresy had popular appeal and was centred on the rejection of the orthodox doctrine of original sin and a belief that humankind had freewill in moral affairs and decisions. Controversially, and this is why the Church feared it so much, the heresy taught human beings could find their own salvation and spiritual truth without the assistance of priests. Pelagius advocated a simple lifestyle based on self-responsibility and the individual's need to choose for themselves how to live their life, without outside interference. These concepts were in direct opposition to the standard teachings of the Church and challenged not only its moral code but also the doctrine of apostolic succession.

Some authorities have seen the Pelagian heresy as a revival of older beliefs. Morgan (1938) goes so far as to say that the heresy was '...in truth nothing else then a revival of druidism and of the old druidic ideas with regard to the nature and freewill of man.' He goes on to say that Pelagianism was so popular and widespread throughout Europe that there was a serious danger of its Christian inhabitants relapsing into their old pagan ways.

The reason for this success seems initially to have been the charismatic personality of the heresy's founder and the eloquence by which he framed his arguments and conducted debates with his opponents. Even his sternest critics admitted he was 'a learned man' who led 'a reproachless life'. The Church found it very difficult to combat and defeat such a persuasive and charming enemy preaching a philosophy that was attractive to many of its new converts The Church's teachings on sin and its repressive morality were difficult for the pagan mind to understand and accept and Pelagianism seemed an interesting and acceptable alternative for many people.

The widespread support for the heresy and its popularity was also causing serious problems of discipline within the ranks of the clergy. Some were attracted to Pelagius and his teachings and joined his followers. Others who had remained loyal to the Church were either arguing among themselves about the heresy or were spending all their time actively campaigning against its spread. For the first time since Christianity became the official religion of the Roman Empire the Church was facing a threat from a serious rival and its moral and spiritual authority was being undermined.

In Britain the heresy had been introduced, says Bede, by Agricola, the son of a Pelagian priest. Bede, not wishing to sound a defeatist note, says the upstanding British naturally rejected the heresy. However the clergy were unable to refute its very plausible arguments or in other words were in a position where they had no defence against it. In 428 or 429, coinciding with Vortigern inviting Horsa and Hengist here, the British Church asked for outside help to combat the heretical menace. A special synod was convened and it was decided to invite two Gallic bishops, Germanus of Auxerre and Lupus of Troye, to Britain as missionaries to re-convert the Christians who had become Pelegians. The two churchmen accepted the invitation and set sail from Gaul across the Channel.

This short sea journey was an eventful one. Bede says when they were halfway across the ship was attacked by devils. These entities were aware the bishops were sailing to England to combat Pelagianism and were determined to prevent them arriving. The demons raised a storm and the sail of the ship was torn to shreds by the fierce winds. Before the ship could go under, Germanus called on Jesus and sprinkled water on the huge waves. Immediately the storm subsided and the intrepid travellers were able to reach the shore safely.

On his arrival, according to Bede, the Gallic bishops travelled up and down the country preaching the true gospel while, at first, 'the authors of false doctrines' (the Pelagian priests) hid from sight. They eventually challenged the bishops and 'appeared with rich ornaments and magnificent robes, supported by crowds of flattering followers.' The Pelagians were allowed to put their arguments first and then Germanus and Lupus addressed the crowd and successfully refuted them. In fact so successful were they, says Bede, in exposing the heretics' lies that the Pelagians were forced to admit their errors. The crowd were so incensed by this climb down that violence was nearly caused to the poor Pelagians.

After this, apparent, success at defeating the heresy the two bishops stayed in Britain for a year. During this time they cured the blind daughter of a tribune (sic) and visited the tomb of St Alban to pay their respects. Bede then claims the Devil caused Germanus to break his leg and while he was recovering in bed some houses next to his lodgings caught fire. Attempts were made to rescue the hapless bishop but the rescuers were beaten back by the flames and heat. Germanus prayed to God and the flames passed over his house and he was unharmed. After this miracle the 'poor folk' gathered in large numbers outside his lodgings begging to be healed by the great man.

In 429 Germanus and Lupus were asked to help defend Britain from the Saxons and Picts. They visited the British army in its camp and baptized many soldiers. Bede says Bishop Germanus actually led the troops into battle and as a result of his spiritual efforts the enemy was scattered and defeated without the spilling of any blood. After this battle the Gallic bishops returned home as their mission had been completed.

This may have been wishful thinking, for Bede reports the Pelagian heresy broke out again and the British bishops were forced to send for Germanus again. He arrived with a new companion, Severus, around 435 and they travelled the country preaching and healing. Germanus soon realised the heretics were in a minority and that most of the people who had been converted were still following the orthodox version of the Christian faith. The 'false teachers' were rounded up and banished by 'common consent' to the Continent where they could 'recognise their errors'. Germanus returned home and died sometime after 444.

Bede is not a reliable observer of the history of the British Church because he was writing from a Romanist viewpoint. It is evident from reading between the lines of the above account that there was considerable and widespread support for the Pelagians and, in having to send for outside help, the Church had failed to stop it and was therefore in a position of some weakness. The synod and the invitation sent to the Gallic bishops was the desperate action of a split and demoralised Church facing both internal heresy and an external pagan threat from the Saxons and Picts.

In his ecclesiastical history Bede leapfrogs the Age of the Celtic Saints and the so-called Arthurian Age, merely remarking that after departure of Germanus the British 'enjoyed a rest from foreign, though not from civil wars'. He says the British (Celts) began to fight among themselves and were guilty of 'unspeakable crimes', including failing to preach the gospel to the Saxons and Angles. This oversight was corrected, says Bede, when God sent 'worthy preachers of truth' in the shape of Augustine's mission at the end of the 6th century.

Bede was born at the end of the 7th century, after the Synod of Whitby had effectively destroyed the power and influence of the Celtic Church. As a monk he had trained under Abbot Benedict Bishop of Wearmouth monastery in Northumbria. Benedict had arrived in Britain from Rome in 669 with Theodore the Greek, who had been appointed as Archbishop of Canterbury by the Pope to suppress the pagan revival and deal with the 'heretics' of the Celtic Church. Bede was therefore a product of the Roman Church and had been shaped in its mould. There are two possible explanations for Bede's lack of interest in the lives of the Welsh Celtic saints. One is that he did not have access to their stories when he was writing his manuscript. This is possible as the life of St David for instance was not written down until the late 11th century. That is the 'cockup' theory of history. The conspiracy theory as it were is that Bede, as a devout Roman Catholic, was not willing to promote the cult of the Welsh saints. However, he did write about the Celtic saints Columba and Aidan and he had met Adamnon, the abbot of the Celtic monastery on Iona and hagiographer of Columba. Bede was present when the abbot visited King Ailfred of Northumbria and adopted 'the Roman usage' or rites used by the Roman Church. On his return to Iona the converted abbot persuaded the others to give up their 'ancient customs' and instructed them in 'the correct ways'. By this example, says Bede, Adamnon restored his followers to the path of Catholic unity.

Despite Bede's omissions from his history of early Christianity, the average person living where the Celtic Church was most active in the 5th or 6th century must have been bumping into saints all the time. Spencer (1990) lists over one hundred and seventy Celtic saints. For space reasons it is not possible to describe the lives of all of them and that is not the purpose of this book. Instead I would like to concentrate in the rest of this chapter and the next two on some of the more important saints who played a role in the Celtic Church and its struggle against the pagan Old Religion. I shall begin with St Dewi or David, the patron saint of my adopted land of Wales.

David was born in 495 and died in 589. He is sometimes known as Dewi Dyfrwr or David the Waterman and this unusual title was given to him because, unlike many of the other saints, he drank only spring water and ignored wine and mead. An alternative theory suggests he was given the title because he led a group of monks known as 'The Watermen'. This elitist group were imitators of the Christian desert hermits and were said to follow the rites of the Coptic Church. This church had been founded at Alexandria in Egypt by St Mark in the 1st century CE. The early Church writer Clement claimed Mark was the author of a 'secret gospel' which was closely guarded within the Coptic Church and could only be read by those initiated into 'the great mystery'. It was claimed that it represented the inner teachings of Jesus which led into 'the innermost sanctuary of the truth'. (Toulson 1987). Alexandria in the first few centuries of the Christian era was a hotbed of heresy, Gnosticism, the Egyptian Mysteries and the occult doctrines known in 16th and 17th century Europe as Hermeticism.

Coptic Christianity influenced the desert hermits and also seems to have found its way to Ireland. Considering the intercourse between Ireland and West Wales, at one stage they were even regarded as one country, it is perhaps not surprising that David and his followers might have been influenced by Coptic beliefs. The gospel of Mark seems to have been based on a less orthodox version of Christianity then the version promoted by the Roman Church. It would have been very attractive to the mystics of the Celtic Church and would explain some of the problems they later had with the Romanists.

The full details of David's life are only known to us because of a manuscript written in 1080 by a monk called Rhygyfarch, who lived at Llanbedan Fawr monastery near Aberystwyth. There are earlier, brief, references to David in the 6th century Irish manuscript known as the Catalogus Sanchorum Hibernia or Catalogue of Irish Saints and in The Martyrology of Tallaght. The latter describes the visit by David, Gildas and Cadog to Ireland and how they celebrated Mass for the Irish saints. (Rees 1990)

In Rhygyfarch's account, David is of royal blood and descended on his paternal side from King Cunneda of Strathclyde, who conquered North Wales in 400. His mother, Non, Nonna or None, was a pagan princess and as her mother was Anna, daughter of Uther Pendragon, she was a niece of King Arthur. If true, this makes David his great-nephew. Non was also said to have been related to the family of the High King Vortigern who had invited the Saxons to sat in Britain.

These alleged royal connections are not unusual in Celtic hagiography. Many of the saints to be described here claimed some form of royal or noble descent. Some of them claimed family links with Arthur, members of his court and warriors of the Round Table Fellowship. These royal associations and links go back to Helen, mother of the Emperor Constantine the Great, who was said to have been a British princess, and her alter-ego Elen of Wales. In the stories where the saints are granted free land by kings and tribal chieftains it is because they themselves are of royal blood or noble ancestry. The rulers were in effect looking after their own.

David's birth was surrounded by strange portents and omens of a pagan nature. His coming was prophesied by Arthur's wizard and spiritual counsellor Myrddin (Merlin) and David's father Prince Sant of Ceredigion, was told by an angel that he would find 'three treasures' concealed in the River Teifi near Cardigan. These were a stag, a salmon and a swarm of bees and were said to relate to the coming birth of the saint. While these have been interpreted as Christian symbols by some writers they also have a pagan significance. The stag is the animal form taken by the Celtic horned god Cernunnos and represents rebirth, healing and the Otherworld. The salmon is a representation of wisdom in Celtic mythology and is associated with pagan sacred springs. Both a stag and a salmon are animal forms taken by the 6th century bard Taliesin after he drank the elixir of transformation from Cerridwen's cauldron of inspiration - the pre-Christian Grail. Bees are an ancient sacred creature of the Goddess.

St Non was raped by Prince Sant and where she lay two standing stones rose out of the earth to mark the spot. When she was ready to give birth Non found 'a special place', which it is sometimes claimed was a cromlech or prehistoric burial mound. Her father jealously plotted to kill the baby, presumably because he did not want an illegitimate heir. As Non gave birth a great storm blew up with thunder, lightning and floods and this protected the mother and baby from harm. An unearthly light, 'as bright as the sun', shone around the birth place and a spring of crystal clear water burst from the ground.

Today the alleged site of the birth can be seen on the cliffs just outside the modern cathedral town of St David's in Pembrokeshire. It is marked by the ruins of a medieval chapel dedicated to St Non. Near to the chapel is a holy well which is also dedicated to her and has her statue in niche. This well is still used for healing purposes . The remains of several standing stones, said to be the remnants of a Bronze Age circle, can be seen in the field surrounding the chapel ruins.

The actual date of the chapel is unknown. It is believed to date from before the 14th century and was abandoned in the mid-16th century, possibly coinciding with the Reformation, when it was transformed into a dwelling house. The chapel has an unusual north-south orientation and in the south-west corner is a stone incised with an equal armed cross. This is a popular pagan symbol that was adopted by the Celtic Church. This stone dates from the 7th-9th centuries and was at one time embedded in the chapel's east wall.

In the Middle Ages Non's well was famous for its healing properties and was visited by people suffering from eye problems and diseases. It can be surmised that the well has a long history dating back to pre-Christian times. An 18th century writer described it as follows: ' There is a fine Well...cover'd with a Stone roof and inclos'd within a Wall, with benches to sit upon around the Well. Some simple people go still to visit this Saint at some particular time's, especially on St Nun's (sic) Day (March 2nd), which they keep holy and they offer Pins, Pebbles etc at this Well'. Judging from the offerings of flowers and coins thrown in the well today it is still being used by not so 'simple people' for healing purposes.

Next to the well and the ruins is a modern chapel built in 1934 by the nearby St Non's Retreat House. It is modelled on the original chapel and is dedicated to Non and the Virgin Mary. It has a very peaceful atmosphere and boasts an altar made from medieval stonework and a stained glass window of the William Morris school depicting David and Non arriving in Brittany.

David was baptised at Porth Clais near his birthplace by his blood relative Aelfyw or Aelvaus, the bishop of Munster in Ireland. A local legend says a spring burst from the rocks to enable the baptism to take place. Some of this water splashed into the eyes of a blind man who was holding the baby during the ceremony and his sight was restored. Here again there are memories of an earlier, pre-Christian healing shrine at a sacred spring.

Non and David left West Wales after the baptism and travelled to Brittany. She stayed and died there but David later returned to his home country. Non is said to have lived at Dirnon - diri is Breton for 'oak' - and lived in a hermitage in the middle of an oak forest. The possibility this was a nemeton or druidic sacred grove cannot be ruled out. A few hundred yards outside the modern town of Dirinon is a spring with a statue of Non. On the third Sunday after Easter and at the end of July (Lughnasadh?) villagers still gather there and march in procession with a cross and banners to the chapel of St Divy (David) where Mass is celebrated.

On his return to Wales David was raised from a young boy to enter the priesthood. He received training at various Christian settlements in Pembrokeshire and Cardiganshire. Several important sites, some with pre-Christian connections are associated with the saint all over West Wales. At Capel y Gwrhyd, about a mile from St David's, is a ruined chapel said to have been used by the saint. It is in a field that was once said to be under a curse. Nothing would grow in it and anyone who attempted to plant crops on the sickened and died. Such stories are fairly common and these 'Devil's Acres', as they often called, were usually former places of pagan worship.

At Penmaen Dewi, or David's Head, there is an old farm called Ty Gwyn or the White House. This is said to have been the site of a monastery founded by St Patrick thirty years before the Welsh saint but later used by both David and his mother. Graves dating from the Celtic Christian period were found here in the 19th century and one of the abbots, called Melgan, is still remembered in the nearby place name of Porth Melgan. Nearby is Ynys Dewi, the Isle of David, now more commonly known as the bird sanctuary of Ramsey Island.

At Pont Cerwyn Dewi the saint is remembered by in the name of a bridge spanning the River Alun. Its name in English means 'bridge of the brewing vat of David'. The word 'cerwyn' can also be found at Moel Cwm Cerwyn in the Preseli hills and Rees thinks the name refers to the magical cauldrons of Celtic myth that never ran dry. She cites as examples the famous cauldron of Cerridwen and the magical cauldron that was one of the Thirteen Treasures of Britain guarded by Merlin. (1992).

At Solva, a few miles south of St David's on the coast, was the Ffos y Mynach or Monk's Dyke. This was an ancient earthwork and according to a 19th century account marked the boundary of sanctuary land where 'felons and every evil person fleeing from place to place' sought refuge. It was also a place where the monks from St David's were not allowed to go which suggests a memory of paganry from earlier times. (Rees 1992)

When he finally became a priest, David rose through the ranks until he became a bishop. Despite this high rank in the Church it is said he followed a simple lifestyle based on the monastic rule. Physically he was a very tall man, over six feet, and was described by his friend Paulinus of

Llandeusant as 'an elegant man, full of grace..he is a loveable man, pleasing in feature, distinguished in form, upright in stature.' He dressed in animal skins and carried a branch as a staff, on top of which hung a magical bell called Bangu or 'the dear loved one'. David also owned a magical horse and one day lent it to a fellow saint who rode it across the Irish Sea. The horse entered the sea and 'ploughed through the swelling mass of waves as if it had been a level field.'

David travelled widely during his lifetime and visited Derbyshire, Somerset, Cornwall and even went abroad to Brittany, Rome and the Holy Land. At Glastonbury, he and seven other bishops built a small church dedicated to the Virgin Mary. This visit and the building of the church is important for it links David with the native British Church of Joseph which the Celtic Christians saw as their parent tradition. At Bath, site of the Roman baths and the Celtic shrine of Sulis-Minerva, David blessed the springs which had become poisoned. One is reminded of events at Bath in recent years where the springs have been closed because of bacterial infections.

One account, possibly legendary, says that David, St Teilo and St Padan visited Jerusalem. There David was greeted as a brother by the Patriarch and was consecrated as a bishop on the Orthodox Church. This story, and his visit to Glastonbury, may have been introduced into his biography for political reasons. They provide David with a legitimacy derived, not from Rome, but directly from a disciple of Jesus and an alternative version of Christian practice and belief.

Sometime between 530 and 540, following the outbreak of the Yellow Plague in Wales, David established a church and monastery on the site of the present 12th century Normal cathedral at St David's. In Celtic Christian times it was known as Mynyw in Welsh and Menevia in Latin. An angel directed David, St Teilo, St Aidan and St Ishmael to the Glyn Rhoslyn or Vale of Rosina, in the upper cwm or valley of the River Alun in what later became known as Dewisland in south-west Pembrokeshire.

At this time most of west Dyfed from south of Aberareon on the north coast, inland to the lower Teifi Valley around Aberteifi (Cardigan), northern Pembrokeshire and western Carmarthenshire had been settled by the Irish. They had intermarried with the native Demetae tribe and established a pagan Celtic kingdom in the region. An inscribed standing stone from Castell Dwyran in Carmarthenshire, now in Carmarthen museum, commemorates the last leader of these Irish-Welsh Celts called Voteporix Proctictoris or Protector. St Gildas, writing in the 540s, denounced him as 'the last tyrant of the Demetae' (Dyfed Archaeological Trust 1986)

The arrival of David and his companions challenged the status quo in the valley. In fact David 'came out fighting' for as soon as he arrived he lit a fire. This was a highly significant gesture to the Celtic tribes people. It was an ancient Celtic law that if someone wanted to possess a epic of common land they had to light a fire on it first. In medieval Welsh law the right to occupy and hold land owned by one's father until one's own death is known as dachannud or 'uncovering the fire'. A squatter on waste land gained possession of it if he could build a house in a night (significantly not the day) and have smoke coming from the chimney by cockcrow at dawn.

As soon as the natives saw the smoke from David's fire they knew they had trouble on their hands. In turn David was aware of his need to stake a claim on the land and also try to win the hearts and minds of the people. The saint encountered serious problems when his right to be in the valley was challenged by the local Irish-Welsh chieftain and druid Boia or Baia. He was totally opposed to the building of a Christian church in his backyard because the valley was sacred to the Old Gods.

Several place names around St David's, such as Pont Clegyr Boia, Fynnon Boia (the well of Boia) and the Rath of Boia, still remain to this day. The chief's settlement was in a disused Iron Age hill fort on the south-west of Cwm Alun called Clegyr Boia. Archaeological evacuations in 1943 revealed it was originally settled in Neolithic times and was a fortified encampment during the Celtic period (Rees 1992). The hill fort was on high ground and overlooked the site chosen by the Christians for their church and settlement.

When Boia saw the smoke from the saints' campfire he became angry that someone should intrude into the valley without his permission. His wife urged him to send out his warriors to deal with the illegal squatters and drive them off the land and out of the sacred valley. Boia realised he had no option and a band of heavily armed warriors left the hill fort to carry out his orders. Before they could reach the monks the men were overcome by a mysterious fever and retreated feeling sick and confused. On their return to the hill fort they found all the cattle and sheep had died while they were away.

Allegedly terrified by these events Boia went out and met with David. He begged the saint for mercy and told him he and his monks could stay in the valley. In return David restored the dead animals to life and good health to his warriors. For a while peace and tranquillity returned to the valley. It was not to last for Boia's wife refused to compromise. She decided that if her partner was too weak to drive the Christians from the valley she would do it instead.

She sent her female servants down into the valley to tempt the monks by bathing naked in the river. In response David fasted against the women. This was an ancient form of Celtic curse adopted by the Church. Accounts differ as to whether the women died or went mad. One chronicler merely says, rather chillingly, ' They walked with the wind upon the path of death.'

By this stage the Celtic chieftain's wife was getting desperate and she decided to invoke the gods of the valley for help in the traditional way. Blinded by her hatred of the Christians, she took her step-daughter on a food foraging trip for hazel nuts into the wooded cwm. They stopped to rest and the older woman offered to delouse the girl's hair. As soon as she laid her head in her lap Boia's wife chopped it off and offered her soul to the Old Gods. Where the blood from the sacrificial victim's severed head fell a spring bubbled up from the earth. This is a common motif in both Celtic pagan and Christian myths and legends and is a survival of the Celt's sacred head cult. This sacred spring was used for healing and it survived into Norman times and was mentioned by Giraldus Cambrensis, or Gerald of Wales, during his famous journey around Wales.

When this ritual sacrifice failed to have the desired effect, Boia's wife allegedly went insane and ran away from the tribe. The druid, distraught at the death of his daughter and the insanity and disappearance of his wife, declared war on the Christian monks. He decided to launch a surprise attack on their camp but, fortunately for them, on the night of the planned attack an Irish raider called Lisci landed on the nearby coast, allegedly at the modern village of Porth Lisci.

He quickly marched inland, attacked the hill fort, bunt all the round houses to the ground and killed Boia. On one account it says that as Lisci attacked a 'fire from heaven' destroyed Boia's tower. Whether this was merely a look-out or maybe a religious structure used by the druid is not known, but it was especially singled out for divine retribution from above.

This story is typical of confrontations between the Celtic missionaries and the pagan tribes at this time. It graphically illustrates the way the Christians arrived in tribal areas, took land and established settlements. Sometimes the saints were lucky enough to have land granted to them by local chieftains or kings who were sympathetic to Christianity or were easily converted. In other cases missionaries were at the receiving end of strong and spirited resistance from the natives who resented both their presence and their attempts to seduce, cajole and threaten them to give up their old forms of worship. This process is frequently glossed over in the clerical histories but it can be easily recognised.

One of the key events in David's life was the famous Synod of Brefi in 545. The site where it took place, later known as Llandewi Brefi or 'church of David on the River Brefi', was a place where several Roman roads met and it therefore allowed easy access from all over West Wales. It appears that by the 540s the old Pelagian heresy was rife again and it was decided to call a synod to deal with it. This meeting was held outdoors and was, allegedly, attended by over one hundred bishops and a multitude of abbots, priests and clergy .

At first David, for some reason, was reluctant to attend until messengers were sent to persuade him to change his mind. On the journey to Brefi David allegedly restored a dead, or perhaps only unconscious, boy to life. The youngster was so grateful for this new lease of life that he converted to Christianity. David allowed the new convert to accompany him to the synod as his loyal servant and disciple.

Once at the gathering David was still strangely reluctant to participate and he refused to address the assembled clerics. Finally the bishops of Caerleon and Bangor managed to persuade him he should speak and

David began to preach to the congregation about the evils of the Pelagian heresy. Unfortunately the crowd was so large that few could see or hear him. David's new disciple laid his shroud on the ground for the saint to stand on. Immediately the earth rose up to form a mound so all could see him and a white dove - symbol of the Holy Spirit - perched on his shoulder. David spoke eloquently against the heresy and all those who heard his words accepted his wise judgement on the matter.

The story of the Synod of Brefi, with all its miraculous trappings, was designed to establish David as the leading bishop in the Celtic Church in Wales and project him as the only cleric who was capable of defeating the powerful Pelagian heresy. It can be directly linked to the stories of his visits to Glastonbury, Rome and Jerusalem which further established his rank and authority in the Church. Strangely he was not recognised as a saint until the 12th century, when ironically it was the Norman bishop of St David's, Bernard, who put his name forward to the Pope.

David's death was surrounded by as many weird portents and omens as his birth ninety four years earlier. He apparently survived at least one attempt to assassinate him. Three monks tried to kill him with bread dipped in poison. David however broke the bread into three portions. One he fed to his dog, one to a raven sitting on the windowsill of his cell and he ate the third. The dog and the raven fell down dead but the saint escaped unharmed. Why the monks should have wanted to kill him remains a mystery. It may represent a power struggle that was going on in the monastery or the wider Celtic Church at that time.

His death in fact came peacefully on March 1st, 589. One morning the monks heard a voice talking to the saint from out of thin air. David informed them afterwards that an angle had told him to prepare for his imminent death. He was told he would die on March 1st and be taken up to heaven by Christ himself with a host of angels. On the third day of the week, at cockcrow, the monastery was filled with a sweet perfume and the singing of angels. At the hour of the morning service Jesus appeared in a vision to David. The saint said: "Take me to thee", closed his eyes and slipped into the sleep of death.

Chapter Five
Pagans & Holy Men

St David's encounter with the native paganism of West Wales was also experienced by the Irish saint Brynach, who arrived in the second half of the 5th century. Brynach was born of wealthy parents and in some accounts is said to have been a chieftain. He abandoned this role however when he went on a pilgrimage to Rome and was converted to Christianity. On the return journey to Ireland he stayed for a while in Brittany before deciding to sail for the western coast of Wales.

He made landfall at the modern site of Milford Haven, now famous for its fishing fleet and its oil refineries, near the estuary of the River Cleddau. Almost as soon as he came ashore Brynach seems to have got himself emotionally entangled with a wealthy Celtic noblewoman who was also a 'wise woman', or priestess, following the Old Ways. Using her knowledge of love potions this woman attempted to seduce the saint from the straight and narrow path of celibacy. The Irishman however was made of sterner stuff. He resisted her physical charms, defeated her magical arts and rejected her romantic overtures.

Frustrated by her lack of success and angered by the saint's lack of interest, the noblewoman hired several local men to hunt Brynach down and kill him. The saint decided all this was getting too much and hastily made plans to leave the area. Before he could escape the hit men caught up with him and one of them stabbed him with a spear. Brynach managed to escape even though he was bleeding profusely. The saint washed the wound at a spring, later called Ffynnon Goch or the Red Well, and immediately the spear wound stopped bleeding and healed over. Afterwards the well was visited by people from all over West Wales seeking cures because of its healing properties.

Brynach realised he had suffered a narrow escape and he sought to put some distance between himself and his attackers. He travelled northwards until he came to the Cwm Gwaun, or Gwaun Valley, near Abergwaun or Fishguard as it is known today. Until the saint arrived in the valley it was infested with witches and evil spirits. He promptly built a church at Pontfaen in the heart of the ancient wooded valley, which contains a primeval wildwood dating back to the Ice Age, and drove out the powers of darkness. In this context it can be assumed the 'evil spirits' were the old pagan gods worshipped by the local tribes. Incidentally, the Gwaun still has a sinister reputation even today and is said to be the haunt of witches, ghosts and goblins.

Brynach also travelled along the River Nevern, past the Pentre Ifan cromlech and into the valley where folk legend says the druids once had their college. At the command of a divine voice, Brynach travelled until he saw a white sow and her piglets on the river bank. At that spot, the voice had said, he should his settlement and build another church. Brynach was granted a llan by the local Celtic chieftain who lived in the hill fort above the modern village of Nevern. The white sow in the story appears in the stories of other saints and is always associated with the siting of a church. In Celtic mythology the white sow was the sacred animal of Cerridwen.

Brynach spent many years living in the Nevern area as a hermit dressed in animal skins and following a vegetarian diet. He dwelt for many years on the nearby Carn Ingli, or Hill of the Angels. This rocky outcrop received its name because of the visions of angelic beings the saint had while he lived on its summit Recently there have been reports of strange phenomena in the Carn Ingli and Nevern areas.

In 1992 there were reports of UFOs or earth lights chasing locals in Nevern village and these small balls of light were seen travelling towards the church and the hill fort In the old days these were known as the Gorff Connwyl or 'corpse candles' and were said to be a premonition of death . These will-o-the-wisp lights were said to hover over the (spirit?) path taken by the coffin from the house to the cemetery. St David is supposed to have asked for God to provide this phenomena so people could see it and prepare for the eternal life. I have also been told by an elderly lady who lives on the slope of Carn Ingli that the locals believe the hill is haunted by faeries and ghosts, including a 'grey lady' and a man on a horse.

The eldest son of Brynach's grand-daughter was St Cadoc or Cadog. His father was a tribal leader in Gwent, South Wales and the saint is sometimes confused with Sir Galahad in the Arthurian legends. As a young man Cadoc was renowned for his wisdom and learning and was called 'Cadoc the Wise'. He had many wise and witty sayings attributed to him, but most of these were apocryphal and already existed in folk tradition.

A famous story links Cadoc and Arthur and describes how the saint gave sanctuary to a man accused of killing three of Arthur's warriors. Cadoc sheltered the man for seven years until Arthur discovered his whereabouts and came seeking revenge. Arthur and Cadoc met on opposite banks of the River Usk, on the border between Wales and England. Cadoc had asked SS Illytd, Teilo and David to judge the case and they had decided the murderer should go free. However, they had also decided that a payment of cattle should be made to Arthur to compensate for the loss of his fighting men.

Arthur thought of a cunning plan to render the judgement invalid. He demanded that the cattle provided by the saint should be red in the front and white in the rear. This strange colouring indicated that the cattle should be of Otherworldly or faery origin. Arthur knew it would be impossible for a Christian saint to obtain these special animals as he could not traffic with the powers of darkness. Unable to meet his obligations Cadoc would have no choice but to give up the killer for punishment.

Cadoc, however, realised the trick the king was trying to pull on him. After all, he was not known as Cadoc the Wise for nothing. He ordered that cattle of all colours should be collected and brought to him. As they were driven past the saint the cattle changed onto the red and white colouring asked for by the king. Cadoc drove the herd to the ford crossing the river where Arthur and his escort, Cai and Bedwyr, were waiting. As the first of the cattle touched the men's hands they turned into bundles of fern. In remorse for attempting to mislead him with pagan tricks, Arthur apologised to the saint and accepted his right to extend sanctuary to the wanted man.

The pagan symbolism in this story is fairly open to see. The transaction between the king and the saint takes place on the border between two countries and across a river, more specifically running water. This siting of the encounter represents the symbolic boundary or crossing-over point between this world and the Otherworld. This is emphasised by the introduction of the faery cattle into the story and their transformation as they cross the river. Strange encounters or ritualised combats at fords are common in folk tradition. The shallowest part of the river symbolically represents the crossing point on this level of reality from the material plane to the spirit world.

Among Cadoc's other notable achievements was teaching the famous bard Taliesin. While he was granted divine wisdom from the cauldron of inspiration in Celtic myth in this version the bard is taught by the Christian saint Cadoc the Wise. This sounds suspiciously like a Christian attempt to gain supremacy over the old pagan beliefs. This is confirmed by the misrepresentation of Taliesin by the Tudor Church as a Christian bard and holy man. When the Saxons began to attack South Wales in large numbers, Cadoc left and went to Brittany. He was later called out of retirement to help the newly converted Celtic Christians resist the influx of paganism imported by the newcomers. The exact circumstances of his death are shrouded in mystery. At least one account says he died a martyr. He was saying Mass when a band of Saxons entered the church and he was killed by one of their spears.

Another Welsh-born saint who is said to have been one of Arthur's warriors of the Round Table was Collen. He was born in mid-Wales and was descended from Caradoc Pendragon who had bravely resisted the Roman invasion and was taken to Rome as a slave in chains. Collen also visited Rome and was involved in a bizarre incident in which he allegedly killed a pagan knight (sic) in front of the Pope. How or why this incident happened is unclear.

Collen, like so many other saints, spent some time in Brittany and built a church there. When he returned to Britain he lived as a hermit in North Wales and Llangollen is named after him. Later he lived as a hermit on the banks of the River Dee. It is his period at Glastonbury which is the most interesting and it provides as with one of the most unusual stories relating to the Celtic saints and their battles with the old beliefs.

In the Age of the Saints Glastonbury was still regarded by many as one of the entrances to the Otherworld. A popular legend states that St Collen did battle with the King of the Faeries who lived on the Tor at this time. In reality this was actually Gwyn ap Nudd, the Celtic god of death and the Wild Hunt. The story begins with Collen deciding to build a hut on the slopes of the Tor and live as a hermit. One dark and windy night he heard two men talking outside the hut about Gwyn and his alleged powers. The saint called out to them to be silent about such matters and they replied he would be chastised for his impudence.

The next day messengers arrived at the hut and invited Collen to visit the King of the Faeries at his palace on top of the Tor or in some versions inside the Tor. Collen politely refused, obviously thinking it would not be good for his image as a hermit, or his future chances of becoming a saint, to be seen socialising with a pagan god of the underworld. The next day another messenger turned up with the same invitation. This time the messenger is dressed in the Otherworldly colours of blue and red. Again the saint made his excuses.

On the third day the messenger returned and this time he was in no mood to accept any of the saint's excuses. He commanded the saint to accompany him to the top of the Tor and warned him that if he did not obey instant death would follow. Now in fear of his life, Collen obeyed but he secretly concealed a vial of holy water in the lining of his robe for extra protection.

Once at the summit of the Tor, Collen saw a castle standing before him shrouded in an unearthly mist. He entered and came face to face with old Gwyn himself, sitting on a golden throne and surrounded by elemental servitors. The Lord of the Underworld invited Collen to sit down and share a meal with him. The saint knew enough about the wiles of the Fair Folk to realise that once he had eaten the faery food he would be under Gwyn's spell. He refused to eat, pulled out the holy water and sprinkled Gwyn with it. There was a clap of thunder and a flash of lightning and the underworld god and his castle vanished in a puff of sulphurous smoke.

This enchanting story illustrates the attitude of the Celtic Church to the old pagan myths. Although many druids had been converted and the cult of the Christian saints was influenced by the mysticism of the old nature religions, the standard line was that pagan worship had to be eradicated and the Old Gods misrepresented as devils. In fact in The Mabinogion the King of the Faeries is described as 'Gwyn ap Nudd, in whom God put the spirit of Annwn (the old Welsh name for the underworld) lest the present world be ruined.' The optimistic conclusion was that with Gwyn banished from the Tor it was no longer an entrance to the Otherworld but just an ordinary hill. Those people who still have odd experiences on the Tor may not agree!

Collen was not the only Celtic saint to have a close encounter with the faery people. A popular folk tale, still recounted on the Welsh Border as late as 1898, describes how St Cadfon was 'travelling between two places' when he got lost. In Cornwall they would still say today he had been 'pixy led'. Luckily he saw some lights shining in the distance and made his way towards them. He discovered the lights were from a house in a wood and when he knocked on the door an old woman answered.

Having heard his story she invited him and provided an excellent meal. Cadfon ate until he was full and began to feel drowsy. The old woman instructed her maid, or young daughter, to show the saint up to the bedroom and there he found the best bed he had ever seen and quickly fell asleep. The next morning he awoke laying on a bed of leaves under the trees. The house and its occupants had vanished. He realised he had been in the Celtic Otherworld and had been entertained by the Queen of the Faeries. In fact there should be no trouble in identifying the old woman and her maid/daughter as aspects of the Goddess. In Celtic myth and fairy tales the Goddess figure often appears to the hero as an ugly old crone who then changes into a beautiful young woman or vice versa.

Yet another Welsh saint who was supposed to have been a knight of the Round Table was Govan or Sir Gawain who had trouble with the jolly Green Knight. Govan was of Irish birth although he lived most of life in Wales. For many years he lived as a hermit at what is now St Govan's Head on the south Pembrokeshire coast and he died in 586. A chapel was later built on the site of his hermit's cell, which is concealed behind the altar in a cleft in the rock. There was a holy well by the chapel visited by people seeking cures for blindness and physical disability as late as the last century. Again this was probably a pre-Christian healing spring.

The most important of the Welsh saints was Illytd or Illtud, sometimes called Illtyd the druid. He was the teacher of other saints such as David, Gildas and Samson and established a famous monastic centre in South Wales. He was of Breton descent and is said to have been either the son of a tribal ruler in Brittany or was born in Breconshire (Powys) of Breton parents. Illtyd left Brittany as a young man to visit his cousin, Arthur, in Britain and he spent some time at his court. Illtyd, and his wife Trynihid, then visited King Poulentus of Morganwg (Glamorgan) and he was made commander of his army.

One day Illtyd and some of the king's men went hunting on land owned by St Cadoc. While Iltyd was absent from their camp hawking the men sent a message to Cadoc demanding he supply them with food for a meal. If he refused they threatened to use force to obtain the supplies. Although Cadoc was angry at their insolence, he sent his monks with the food. The hunters sat down to eat it and immediately the earth opened up and swallowed them.

When Illtyd arrived back at the camp and saw what had happened he was horrified. He went to the saint and asked his advice on what he should do. The holy man replied that he should give up his military career and henceforth devote his life to God and the spiritual path. On hearing this advice, Illtyd rode back to the king, explained what had happened and resigned as commander of the army.

Accompanied by his wife and servants, Illtyd left the court and rode until nightfall. The travellers arrived on the banks of the River Nadwan and constructed a temporary shelter from reeds gathered from the riverside. During the night Illtyd had a dream and was told by an angel to travel west and establish a permanent residence in a wooded valley he would find. The angel also warned him that a man who loved his parents or his wife more then god could never be a true believer.

The next morning when Illtyd got up he saw his wife returning naked from feeding the horses. He immediately despised her, the chronicler says, and ordered her to get dressed and leave the camp. Some time after this it is reported that she visited the saint unannounced and as a punishment lost her eyesight. Illtyd however felt sorry for her and restored it with his healing touch.

At a place called Hadnant the saint found the wooded valley mentioned by the angel. It was full of springs feeding brooks that flowed into a river and populated with all kinds of animals and birds. Iltyd was visited by St Dyfrig, who received his confession and gave him a penance for all the dark deeds he had committed in the past. Illtyd shaved off his warrior's beard and long hair and adopted the tonsure and habit of a monk. He built a church in the woods and lived for many years as a hermit.

Shortly after Illtyd took up residence in the wood King Merchiaun Vesanus, or as he was sometimes known Merchiaun the Mad, was out hunting and chased a stag into the copse where the saint was building his church. The terrified animal was chased by the dogs into the saint's bedchamber where it took refuge. When the king arrived he was annoyed to find the saint in situ and demanded he give up the stag to his hounds. Illtyd refused and after some heated discussion the king granted a reprieve to the stag and told the saint he could stay on his land.

Illtyd tamed the stag and it was employed to pull a wagon full of timber for the church building. Giraldus Cambrensis, writing in the 12th century, records that the stag and Illtyd's horse mated. A foal was born which had the front half of a horse and the back half of a deer. Another legend says a golden stag, presumably some king of effigy, was buried facing west (the direction of the underworld in Celtic mythology) outside Llantwit Major, formerly Llan Illtyd. It is said if the stag is ever found the town will be restored to prosperity and glory. Illtyd's connection with the stag suggests the wood he settled in may have been a pagan sanctuary, possibly dedicated to Cernunnos, the stag god of the forests who was associated with prosperity, fertility and the underworld (the Hollow Hill).

Illtyd's relationship with King Merchiaun was stormy one. Eventually an angel visited the king in a dream and warned him that anyone who interfered with the saint, of whatever social rank, would be destroyed. When the steward of the royal household tried to force the saint to pay tributes to the king he was punished by God and his body 'melted like wax before a fire.' The king then tried to kill Illtyd but he fled to a cave on the River Gwenni, where he was visited by angels and fed with fish and bread from Heaven. After a while the saint returned to his woodland church and the king was killed by being swallowed up by the earth.

Sometime between 470 and 480 Illtyd abandoned his hermit existence and founded a teaching monastery at what is now Llantwit Major. His pupils included David, Gildas and Samson and missionaries from the monastery travelled all over Wales, Cornwall and Brittany. Illtyd was described by his contemporaries as 'a learned man' and he was 'skilled in geometry, grammar, mathematics and all the arts of philosophy'. It is possible he may have received some druidic training as a young man or even came from an hereditary druidic background. It was said he was '..by descent a most wise magus (magician), druid and fore knower of future events'.

In the 8th century Marvels of Britain by Nennius it is claimed Arthur's body was handed over to Illtyd for safekeeping. One day the saint was praying in a sea-cave when a boat floated in bearing two old and wizened men with long grey hair and beards. Also on the boat was the body of a warrior wrapped in a purple cloak and above it an altar was suspended in the air. When Illtyd queried the meaning of this intrusion into his meditations one of the boatmen told him: "This man of God charged us to bring him to thee and to bury him with thee and how thou shouldst not reveal his name to anyone, lest men should swear by him'.

This is obviously a Christian alternative to the pagan myth of Arthur's body being carried off by the three queens, the Triple Goddess, to the Isle of Avalon or the Celtic underworld. Iltyd died between 530 and 545 and allegedly the mysterious body was buried in the same tomb.

One of Illtyd's pupils was St Samson, who was born in Gwent in South Wales and lived from 480 to 560. He was the son of high-ranking nobles who had been foster-parents to the princes of Dyfed and Gwent. Samson's parents had consulted a holy man or druid because they could not have children. He told Samson's father to make a silver rod equal in length to his wife and offer it to God. This would enable them to have a child. The rod is obviously a sacrificial offering symbolically representing the wife.

That night the couple stayed at the holy man's house and the wife had a dream in which an angel told her that he firstborn would be a 'high priest' and seven times brighter then the silver rod. She was to call him Samson after the Biblical character. The next morning, before she could tell the druid, he related a similar dream during which he was told he would be

Samson's teacher. This 'druid' must be Illtyd who later taught Samson at his monastery.

As a priest Samson was renowned for his fight against the old paganism. In one story he crossed swords with an old woman who had eight sisters, all followers of the Old Ways. The saint challenged the woman to abandon her beliefs and when she refused he struck her down dead. Samson's battle with an old witch with ' grey shaggy hair, red garments and holding a trident' has been interpreted as a representation of the Triple Goddess of the Celts or one of her priestesses. (Ross 1967). In another story, Samson visited Cornwall and found the natives worshipping a pagan idol. At first they refused to stop until a boy fell from his horse and lay as if dead. Samson told the pagans his god had the power to restore the boy back to life. They promised to stop worshipping the idol if the saint could perform this miracle and when he did they all converted.

Several of the Celtic Christian saints have associations linking them with the pagan Celtic cult of the sacred or severed head. The Celts were head hunters who kept the skulls of their enemies as trophies and they regarded the head as the sacred centre of the body and the repository of the soul. One of the saints associated with this cult was Teilo. He was a cousin of David and had been born near Tenby on the south Pembrokeshire coast. He was trained at first by the monks on Ynys Byr or Caldey Island, then became a student at Illtyd's monastic school and finally he was the abbot of Bangor Deilo at Llandaff.

The story of Teilo studying with the Caldey monks and then graduating to Llan Illtyd seems to be supported by some archaeological evidence linking the island's early Christian settlement with Illtyd. The evidence in question is the Caldey Stone, a standing stone carved with a Christian cross and inscribed with both Ogham and Latin lettering. The inscription refers to St Dyfrig and is described as Magl Dubr. This is from the Gaelic Mael Doburahan, meaning a 'water-dog' or otter. Some authorities have also identified Illtyd's name on this stone. Certainly the saint, Samson and Dyfrig are all known to have lived on Caldey at various points on their lives. (Bushell 1908).

Geoffrey of Monmouth claims Teilo was originally called Helios, the Greek sun god, because of his strong virtue and wisdom. Such an unusual name for a child suggests his parents might have been pagans. In 547, when the dreaded Yellow Plague swept across the land, Teilo left Wales and visited both Cornwall and Brittany for seven years. On his return he used his power of cursing to help the Welsh drive back the Saxons who had breached the defences at Wye. He died at Llandeilo, 'the church of Teilo', where there is a holy well dedicated to him in a grotto almost under the churchyard.

At another healing well dedicated to the saint at Maenclochog in Pembrokeshire medieval pilgrims drank water from a skull said to be a relic of the saint. This unusual drinking vessel was kept safe by the Melchoir family, who were hereditary guardians of the well and owned the land upon which it stood. The use of the skull to drink the well water was essential for the cure to work. In the last century a gentleman drove down from Swansea by horse and carriage to cure his son of tuberculosis. He neglected to use the skull to give the boy the water and his condition worsened. He had to return to West Wales and complete the ritual properly before the child began to improve. I visited the site several years ago but the farmhouse was empty, the well was overgrown and the skull was nowhere to be found. Rumour had it that the practice died out in the 1920s, when the last of the family died, and the strange drinking vessel disappeared.

St Winifrede or Gwenfrewi was born in North Wales and is another Celtic saint associated with the head cult. She was a young virgin and was pursued by Prince Caradoc ap Alyn who wanted her hand in marriage. They met by accident one day on a hill above a church and the prince asked her to marry him. He threatened that if she refused he would kill her. Winifrede was not interested in his proposal and in attempt to escape his clutches she ran to the church seeking sanctuary.

The prince caught up with her and repeated his offer of marriage and the threat that accompanied it if she did not concede to his wishes. Winifred replied she was already married to a king (Jesus?) and was not interested in his offer. When she further resisted, the prince grew angry, drew his sword and beheaded her. As if by magic where Winifrede's head and blood fell to the earth a spring bubbled up out of the ground.

This vicious murder was witnessed by Winifred's uncle, St Beuno, who had come running out of the church when he heard the argument outside. He picked up his niece's head and cursed the prince, who promptly fell down dead on the spot and the earth swallowed him up. Beuno replaced Winifrede's head on her shoulders and restored her back to life. She was so grateful that she immediately converted to the Christian faith.

Winifrede became an abbess and was buried in the churchyard at Gwytherin near Llanwrst. In 1138 her remains were unearthed and interred at Shrewsbury Abbey. Her shrine was destroyed during the Reformation, although a few relics allegedly of the saint are still preserved in the abbey and at the Roman Catholic convent at Holywell. Pilgrim's still visit St Winifrede's holy well for healing.

Her uncle, St Beuno, is associated with the 11th century church dedicated to him at Pistyll on the Lleyn peninsula in north-west Wales. The church is on the old pilgrim route to Ynys Enlli or Bardsey Island (the Isle of the Bards?) and was built within a circular llan or enclosure of pre-Christian date. The present churchyard wall is oval and next to the church is a holy well with a reputation for healing dedicated to Beuno. The church itself had a thatched roof until the 1840s and has an ancient font described in the guide leaflet as 'of Celtic origin'. It is carved with symbols depicting 'life without beginning or end'. Outside in the churchyard, the guide informs, grow dwaleberries which are 'reputed to possess (the) power to assist in the transmigration of souls.' This can be interpreted as either shape shifting or reincarnation and in the olden times dwaleberries were used for spirit travelling.

The water in the holy well is still used for baptisms and since 1969 the ancient practice of decorating the church with medical herbs and strewing the floor with herbs and rushes has been revived. This is only done for special services at Christmas (the winter solstice), Easter (the vernal equinox) and, as the guide says, 'the early August Lammas festival.' I was lucky enough to be taken to see this church by Keith Morgan and Anna Greenslade of the neo-pagan magazine The Deosil Dance in early 1993. The church was still decorated with dying vegetation and the stone floor was covered in aromatic herbs and rushes. The feeling was like stepping back in time 1500 years to the period when the Celtic saints lived.

The third Celtic saint associated with the head cult was Decuman. Born in the 6th century he was educated by Celtic monks and ended up as a missionary in Somerset at the time when it was invaded by pagan Saxons. His attempt to convert them were violently resisted and saint was attacked and beheaded. He calmly picked up his head and walked over to a nearby spring where he washed it clean of blood. From that day on the spring had a reputation for healing. The saint then decided to sail to Wales to escape the Saxons. He crossed the Bristol Channel and landed in Dyfed. Where he rested his head another spring burst from the ground and became famous for its healing powers. Decuman returned to Somerset where he had the bad luck to be martyred again. This time he did not survive and died.

Several of the minor Welsh saints had legendary lives suggesting they may have been either originally pagan gods or goddesses or took on their mythical attributes. St Melangell, for example, is said to have been praying in her woodland retreat when the Prince of Powys rode into the clearing chasing a large hare. The animal hid under Melangell's skirts and refused to come out. The huntsman raised his horn to summon his hounds but the instrument stuck to his lip. Since that day nobody has dared hunt or kill a hare in the area.

In 1993 The Independent newspaper reported that hundreds of pilgrims are still visiting St Melangell's church at Llangynog in mid-Wales. A book of supplications is kept in church for people to write their requests for healing for anything from alcoholism to leukaemia. The church stands on the site of a 2000 year old Bronze Age sanctuary and is surrounded by ancient yew trees. The hare, of course, was a sacred animal to the Celts and in folklore and mythology was associated with witches and the moon goddess.

St Dwynwen was the daughter of St Brynach and was the patron of love and healing. In the 14th century the poet Dafydd ap Gwilym burnt candles in front of her 'golden image' at Llandwyn on Anglesey and asked her for help with his love affairs. At her holy well -known as the Cauldron of Dwynwen - people gathered for healing from miles around. In the 1800s an old woman, who was the guardian of the well, practised divination by casting the client's handkerchief on the top of the water and then observing the movement of the tiny eels in the well below. If the water bubbled up in the 'Cauldron' during this ritual it was said the enquirer would have a successful love affair.

In south Glamorgan the saint was linked to a natural rock formation in the shape of an arch to be found in a sea-cave. This was know as the Bow of Destiny and lovers threw pebbles over it to indicate the number of years before they would marry. The legend says that Dwynwen left her bow on the beach and the Hag of the Night (!?) transformed it into the stone arch. Dwynwen's symbols are a bow, a girdle and the crescent moon. G.R. Henken (1987) has seen this saint as a Christianised version of the Roman moon goddess Diana combined with the goddess of love, Venus. Farming families in North Wales offered prayers to Dwynwen as the protector of animals, especially livestock, until the end of the 18th century.

St Mabon was the son of Teilo but some authorities identify him with Mabon ap Modron in The Mabinogion, the 'shining one' who was son of the Celtic 'divine mother' goddess Modron or Matrona. Male pilgrims visiting his holy well at Llanfabon used the waters as a scrying mirror to see the reflection of their future partner's face. In *The Mabinogion*, Mabon assists a young man to find a bride.

The Irish saint Tathan came to Wales in the 5th century and established a monastery at Caerwent in South Wales. When he stepped ashore a stag trotted out of the woods and held the mooring rope of his boat in its mouth. Later the stag knelt in homage to the saint and offered his body for the monks to eat their first meal on Welsh soil. Tathan was known as 'the father of the woods' and possibly may have been a Christianised version of Cernnunos/Herne. Alternatively the stag's homage to the saint may reflect how he converted a tribe who were worshipping the old stag god of the forest.

Tewdric was a 6th century prince of South Wales who became a hermit. When the Saxons invaded he left his spiritual retreat to help fight them. As a result he received a fatal head wound and was carried in a cart drawn by two stags to a holy well near Newport, Gwent. The well contained a log which floated on the water and was large enough for several men to stand on. Every year the high spring tide carried the log out to sea an and it stayed there until the next tide washed it back in again.

A local historian and writer, A. R. Ulting, suggested in 1985 that this folk story was connected in some way with the Germanic earth goddess Nerthus. He regarded Twedric as a 'divine king' sacrificed to the Goddess to bring fertility to the crops. In Celtic tradition the sacred king symbolically mated with the goddess of the land, or her human representative, and after seven years was ritually killed so his blood could fertilise and renew the earth. While this theory may be a little far-fetched there is an old earthwork near the holy well which may be the remains of a pagan sanctuary and the first part of the saint's name, Tew, is the name of the Northern European war god Tew or Tyr.

The last Welsh saint we will look at in this chapter is Dubricius or Dyfrig, who was born in 460 and died in 546. He was of royal birth and came from Herefordshire on the Welsh Border. At that time Herefordshire was part of Wales and in fact it is only until comparatively recently that it ceased to be Welsh speaking.

Dyfrig was the founder and patron of several religious schools and helped establish Celtic Christianity in Wales. He originally resided at a place called Mochros, or 'the place of the pigs'. This place name comes from the legend that an angel visited him and told him to build his church at a place where he saw the lair of a white sow and her piglets.

Another legend says Dyfrig officiated at the coronation of the young Arthur and in fact was present when he drew the sword from the stone. He was allegedly said to be Arthur's uncle which makes him either the brother of Uther Pendragon or Ygraine of Cornwall. During his lifetime Dyfrig was bishop of Llandaff and, with Samson, founded the monastery on Bardsey. He retired there and lived as a hermit before dying and being buried on the traditional 'Island of Saints'. Churches are dedicated to this saint in Radnorshire, Herefordshire and Somerset. In 1120 his bones were removed from Bardsey and reburied at Llandaff.

So far we have discussed the Welsh and Breton saints but there was also a flourishing Celtic Church in Kernow or Cornwall. In the 5th and 6th centuries Cornwall became isolated from Wales (in Celtic times it was even sometimes called 'West Wales') by the new Saxon kingdom of Wessex. There was however still the sea route between northern Cornwall and South and west Wales and the Celtic Church there also had strong links with Brittany. Celtic Christianity developed in Cornwall along the same lines as elsewhere, with a tradition of monastic centres and hermitages and missionary monks who layer became saints.

As elsewhere the lives of the saints were written at a later date and they suffered the same exaggerations and excesses of clerical bias and distortion. The hagiographers painted the pagans as devils incarnate and the saints as miracle-making holy men if impeccable moral virtue. However there seems to have been a strong hermit tradition in Cornwall and these solitary mystics would have inherited some aspects of the old paganism. They acted a light keepers, beacon lighters and guardians of holy wells and sacred springs.

One of the most famous of these Cornish saints was Nectan who lived near Tintagel, the legendary birthplace of Arthur. St Nectan is said to have been a monk at Glastonbury who left the settlement there to seek a life of mystical solitude in the west. St Nectan's Glen is a popular tourist attraction today with a tea shop and an entrance fee to the famous waterfall and pool where the saint's hermitage once stood. The wooded walk up the glen sometimes has a strange atmosphere and is said to be haunted by faeries and elemental spirits. The waterfall is said to be a mist-gate. or gateway to the Otherworld, and Earth Mysteries writer Robin Ellis claims this site can be linked with the weird manifestations in other parts of Cornwall of cryptozoological creatures such as the Owl man, mermaids and the famous Cornish sea serpent.

One of the other Cornish saints, Neot, has possible pagan connections. He was related to the West Saxon kings and had also studied at Glastonbury. Neot lived in a hermitage by a spring now known as St Neot's Well near Hamstoke. There were also two pools near the well, possibly overflows of the main water supply. One of these had three fish in it who provided the saint's meal every day and were then magically replaced overnight. It was also said the saint stood in the pool to recite his prayers. Both these stories sound like survivals of Celtic water worship.

There are numerous holy wells and sacred springs throughout Cornwall and many of these are connected with the lives of Celtic saints and have healing powers. In post-Christian times these sometimes became 'wishing wells' in a folk memory of their original use for sacrificial offerings to the

Old Gods. These wells were more often used for healing, as at Madron on the Lizard peninsula. When I visited this site some years ago there were many pieces of clothing, including Marks & Spencer underwear, hanging from branches around the well left by those seeking healing as offerings.

Several of the Welsh saints were connected with Cornwall and either lived there or visited it on missionary work. These included St David, who is remembered in a church dedication at Davidstow near Bodmin Moor, SS Cubert of Gwbert and St Breoc, both from Cardigan, SS Kenwyn and Mabyn, who were daughters of St Brynach, St Mawgan of South Wales, St Piran, who became the patron of tin miners with St Joseph (of Arimathea) and St Samson, who banished a serpent god worshipped by local pagans. There also references to several Irish saints who made brief visits.

One of the most important early Christian sites in Cornwall is St Michael's Mount. This was a Celtic Christian monastery and may originally have been a druidic college. It was known to the Romans as the Island of Ictis, to the Celts as Dinsul - the citadel of the sun -and to the medieval Cornish as Karrek Iuz en Kuz or 'the hoar (old) rock in the wood'. The Welsh called it Mon Tumba or Twmp, meaning a prehistoric burial mound. It gets its Christian name from a vision seen by fisherman on the rock of the Archangel Michael.

It is possible the popular cult of St Michael in Cornwall an Somerset replaced an earlier cultus of pagan sun worship (Taylor 1916). There are interesting links between St Michael's Mount and the Mont de St Michel in France. The latter is the site of a shrine to the Black Madonna, a Christian representation of the Dark Goddess, and she is called the Notre Dame de Mont Tombe. The last word is a German diminutive of the Welsh (Celtic) twmp (Taylor 1916). To add the seasoning to this heady pagan stew, St Michael is also the patron saint of the Cornish town of Helston. The famous fertility ritual of the Helston Furry Dance is held on the saint's feast day of May 8th every year.

Chapter Six
The High King, the Saint and the Goddess

In this chapter I propose to describe the lives of two of the most famous Irish saints, Patrick and Brigid. Although claimed by the Irish as their patron saint, Patrick or Patricius was a 5th century Romano-British subject who was kidnapped by Irish pirates. There is some confusion as to who the real historical Patrick was and there are several claimants. It is said Patrick's real name was Succath and he was born in northern Britain to a Romano-Celtic family. He had a Christian background and his father, Calpurnius, was a deacon and his grandfather, Pontitus, was a priest.

At the age of sixteen, Patrick and his sister were captured by pirates who killed his father and carried the boy off to Co. Antrim. Patrick became a slave in the household of Milchu, the chieftain of the Dalriada, a Celtic tribe who also inhabited southern Scotland, and he spent six years as a cattleherd. When he was twenty three Patrick heard a voice telling him he would soon return to his own country. Later he had a dream in which he was shown a ship waiting at the coast for his return. Patrick escaped captivity, made his way to the waiting ship and sailed to Gaul.

His enforced stay in Ireland had filled Patrick with a missionary zeal to convert the Irish . In 432 he returned to the country with a band of companions and landed near the modern town of Wicklow. According to the 8th century Life of St Patrick by Muirchu, an Irish druidic prophecy had foretold '..the coming of a foreign religion in the manner of a kingdom with a certain strange and lawful doctrine across the seas, proclaimed by a few, accepted by the many and honoured by all; one that would overturn kingdoms, slay kings that resisted it, lead away multitudes, destroy all their gods and, having cast down all the resources of their Art, will reign for ever and ever'. Patrick's arrival saw the prophecy begin to come true.

After a short rest Patrick and his fellow missionaries sailed along the coast until they arrived at Stangford Lough. Here they encountered a local chieftain called Dichu Finn, who apparently was so impressed by Patrick that he became the first Irish person to be baptised. Dichu presented the ground they were standing on to the saint as a gift to build the first Irish church. Patrick then set off for the homestead of Milchu to confront his old master. He had heard of the saint's arrival and burnt himself to death in his house rather then accept conversion. Patrick arrived, found his plan had been thwarted and put a curse on Milchu's family. He declared they should never own land again but would always be the subjects of others and this came to pass.

Patrick then returned to Stangford Lough to prepare for his assault on the druidic power centre at Tara and his struggle to gain supremacy over the Old Ways. Patrick knew that if he was to convert the Irish he first had to defeat the druids. Tara was the symbolic omphalas or heart of the land where five ancient roads met and it was dedicated to the goddess Tea (Ross 1967). It was not far from the Boyne valley, site of the famous megalithic mounds of Newgrange and Knowlth which feature in Irish Celtic mythology. Tara was also the traditional crowning place of the high kings of Ireland. Like all the Celtic missionaries, Patrick knew that if he could defeat the pagan priests and then convert the aristocracy the common people would be forced to conform.

Patrick decided to launch his attack on Tara on Easter Eve and he and his followers deliberately lit their paschal fire in the area. The high king, Loigaire, and his druids and nobles were assembled at Tara to light their own sacred balefire to celebrate the beginning of spring. It was the ancient custom that no other fire should be lit in the land until the ritual fire at Tara had been kindled by either the king or his archdruid. The Christian missionaries assembled on another hill adjacent to the sacred centre and lit their fire in defiance of this custom.

When the high king saw the other fire in the distance he consulted his druids. They were naturally worried about this open defiance of the Old Ways and told him: "Unless this fire is quenched this same night, it will never be quenched and the kindlier of it will overcome us all and seduce all the folk of your realm." The king replied that if this was true the kindlier of the fire would pay for this act with his life. He ordered nine chariots to be prepared and he, his queen, two druids and a contingent of troops set out for the other hill in battle order.

As the war party approached the hill where the Christians were waiting, the druids warned the king not to enter the circle formed by the fires lit by the monks. They told him that once inside he would be in the power of the Christian saint. Instead they advised the high king to summon Patrick to his presence outside the ring of fire. They also recommended that none of the party should rise as the saint approached or they would come under his spell. One of the king's boy servants did rise and he was instantly converted and later became a bishop in the Irish Celtic Church.

One of the druids, named Lochru, began to verbally abuse Patrick and his faith. The saint invoked God and the druid was lifted up into the air and flung down on a nearby boulder smashing his skull. At this outrage the high king ordered his bodyguard to seize Patrick and kill him. The saint began to chant: " Let God arise and let his enemies be scattered. Let them that hate God flee before his wrath." Immediately, and for no apparent reason, the king's warriors began to fight among themselves. Then, when an earthquake began to shake the ground, they dropped their weapons and fled in terror.

With his chief druid dead and his soldiers scattered, the king was left defenceless. His queen interceded on his behalf and begged Patrick not to kill her husband. She promised he would give up his pagan beliefs and worship the saint's god instead. The king agreed even though he was also secretly plotting to kill Patrick and his monks at the first chance. The saint received a premonition of this plan and he transformed himself and his monks into stags so they could escape.

The following morning, Easter Day, the king was entertaining his nobles at his palace at Tara when Patrick and his companions materialised in the hall, even though all the doors were closed and guarded. A druid called Lucetmael offered the saint a cup of mead, into which he had slipped a drop of deadly poison. Patrick blessed the drink and the liquid froze into solid ice. He tipped the cup over and the unfrozen drop of poison dribbled out. He then blessed the cup again and the ice melted so he could drink it safely.

Lucetmael then challenged Patrick to demonstrate his magical powers. The druid cast a spell to make it snow and it fell until it was almost waist high. Patrick challenged him in turn to melt the snow but Lucetmael said it would not go for twenty four hours. The saint laughed and said: " So druid, you can do evil but not good" He blessed the snow and it melted away at his touch.

Patrick then challenged the druid to an ordeal by fire. A hut was constructed made of half green wood and half dry wood. One of Patrick's monks was placed in the dry half, wearing the druid's robe, while the pagan priest went into the green half, wearing Patrick's robe. The hut was the set alight and the saint began to pray. The druid was burnt alive, leaving Patrick's robe intact, while the monk walked unharmed from the flames with the druidic robe burnt to a cinder.

The high king was impressed by this miracle but still refused to accept Christianity as his religion. He did however compromise and he agreed not to interfere with Patrick's mission and to protect him while he was in the kingdom. When he died the king was buried with his arms crossed over his chest in the pagan fashion and on his dying orders no cross was raised above his tomb.

Following his failure to convert the high king, although he had seriously weakened the power and authority of the druids,, Patrick set out on a series of missionary expeditions across Ireland. While he was under the protection of the high king nobody, warrior or druid, could harm him although the Celtic priests did take other action to harass him as we shall see.

Patrick's first stop was at Connaught, where the high king had sent his two daughters to be raised by two druids who were brothers. The daughters were called Ethne the White and Feidelen the Red. These are, of course, colours associated in Celtic lore with the underworld and the Goddess. As the women were receiving druidic training they may have been destined to become priestesses. The druids wanted to protect them from Patrick and they conjured up a thick mist to hinder his journey. This mist remained for three days and nights until Patrick, realising it had been created by druid magic, prayed until it dispersed.

Ethne and Feidelen were in the habit of rising at dawn and bathing at a local well. They were surprised one morning to find Patrick and his monks sitting by the well praying and reading the scriptures. The women, who are described as virgins, pestered the saint with questions about his faith and his god. After they had heard his replies, the women asked Patrick to teach them. He told them to renounce their 'evil ways ' and he baptised them in the well.

Afterwards the converts asked if it was possible to see the face of Jesus. The saint gave a curious reply: " You cannot see the face of Christ, except you taste of death and except you receive the sacrifice.' The women responded: " Give us the sacrifice so that we may behold our Son." Patrick administered the eucharist and it is recorded the women 'slept in death'. Their bodies were buried in a circular ditch and a church was built over the site. The two druid brothers also converted and became monks who looked after the church This is a very odd story and it is rich in pagan symbolism. We have two virgin priestesses of the Goddess receiving instruction from two druidic brothers. The women are engaged in some kind of dawn ritual at a sacred spring. They are then converted, ritually killed and buried as some kind of foundation sacrifice at a pagan site on which a church is built. The druids become monks and guardians of this sacred site.

While he was staying at Connaught, Patrick encountered the worship of an ancient god called Crom Cruach. This deity was worshipped in the form of an anthropomorphic idol covered in gold and silver. This image stood in the centre of a circle of standing stones and the firstborn of animals and humans were sacrificed to Crom to ensure a good harvest. Every year at Samhain (November 1st) the high king came from Tara to worship Crom, who was regarded as the oldest of the Irish gods. Considering his connection with the harvest and when his major festival was celebrated, he may have been an ancient pre-Celtic fertility god of the dead.

Patrick moved swiftly to stamp out the cult of Crom. Ignoring the protests from the natives, he led a procession of his monks into the stone circle and struck the image of the fertility god with his staff. It immediately began to

94

crack an it toppled over and fell into pieces. As Crom's worshippers watched in astonishment the fallen stones slowly crumbled to dust. They were so impressed by this Christian magic that they abandoned the pagan ways and put their faith in the new religion. The saint also visited and preached at Emain Macha, near Armagh. This was still an important tribal and religious centre of Ulster in the 5th century and had been founded nearly a thousand years before.

Archaeologists investigating the site have found the remains of a mound and earthwork used for ritual purposes and dating back to the 1st century BCE. They also found a sacrificial pool of the Bronze Age period This pool contained the remains of domestic animals and humans. Ironically, in 1993 the site was transformed into an archaeological theme park and museum with funds provided jointly by the Roman Catholic Church and the Church of Ireland.

In his old age Patrick gave up his teaching and preaching and retired to Britain, where he spent his last days at Glastonbury where he was buried.. Some say he imposed the monastic rule on the hermits who were living at St Joseph's original settlement and became the first abbot of Glastonbury. When he died in 464 Patrick's burial place became a pilgrimage shrine. In the 7th century a group of Irish pilgrims visiting his grave were killed by local pagans and became martyrs. Although Patrick is obviously a Celtic Christian saint who is totally opposed to the druids and the old paganism, the image presented of him in the ancient annals is surprising. Patrick is presented as some kind of quasi-druid fighting pagan wizardry with his own powerful brand of Christian magic. In his battles with the Old Religion he challenges the druids to magical combat and wins. Those who oppose him either suffer his death curses or die violently by the wrath of God.

The impression given in his life story is that Patrick defeated the druids and destroyed the old paganism. The legend that he drove out all the snakes from Ireland is said to represent his expulsion of the druids, who were popularly known as 'the serpents of wisdom'. However, as in the rest of the British Isles, many of the country folk only paid lip-service to the new religion and their promises to obey the Christian priests. In reality the old beliefs lingered on and they still survive even today under the surface of rural life.

It was not until 637, nearly two hundred years after Patrick's death, that the Irish Church was strong enough to finally crush the druids. In that year the practice of druidism was finally prohibited and the pagan priesthood was abolished. There is however plenty of evidence to support the claim that remnants of the druidic cultus survived in folk tradition as late as the 16th century. It is also believed to have survived in the secretive Celtic Christian sects of the Culdees or 'Companions of God' who wore druidic white robes and adopted pagan symbols. (Spence 1928). An 11th century Archbishop of Canterbury spoke out against the Irish Culdees and their 'heathen ways'. Stories were told that they carried out sacrifices in the druid manner to propitiate the powers of darkness (the old pagan gods). When Giraldus Cambrensis visited a Irish Culdee monastery on an island at Monincha he described it as 'a church of the old religion'.

The early Irish Church in general observed some of the former customs of pagan Celtic society where they did not conflict with Christianity. The moral code of the Church however was in direct opposition to pagan morality . The early Christian laws on marriage, for instance, gave little consideration to a basically pagan society where divorce, second marriages and concubines were widely accepted as normal.

The celibate monks enforced a strict moral code demanding that both partners in marriage had to remain faithful. If a wife left her husband he was not allowed to remarry and if she returned she had to act as his slave as a penance. If a wife was rejected by her husband she could not remarry or take a lover and had to live a celibate life until she died. Even within marriage certain times of the year, coinciding with religious festivals, were allocated for sexual abstinence.

This repressive moral code was difficult for the pagans to accept for in the older religions sexuality was regarded as a sacrament and religious rites to increase the fertility of crops, animals and humans were a prominent feature of the cycle of seasonal festivals. As late as the 17th century Irish bishops complained about the sexual antics of the country folk on the old Celtic festivals. They condemned the invocation of devils, the reciting of 'cursing prayers' and pilgrimages to holy wells as the survival of pagan habits. Midsummer fires were also still being lit on hilltops on St John's Eve (June 23rd) in a custom dating back to ancient sun worship. It is true some of the pagan priests and priestesses remained virgins or practised celibacy, but this was a matter of personal choice for valid spiritual reasons and was not forced on the majority of devotees.

The cult of Patrick ironically attracted and preserved many aspects of the old beliefs and practices. Many people though St Patrick's Day (March 17th), coinciding with the vernal equinox a few days later, officially marked the beginning of spring. On this day it was said the saint took the 'cold stone' out of the water where he had placed it at Samhain. From St Patrick's Day it was said the weather would improve as winter's cold was banished. Patrick became associated with many holy wells which are still being patronised for healing purposes. At Streull Wells in Downpatrick it is said the saint blessed the wells and is buried nearby, not at Glastonbury. Each of the wells has different healing properties and are visited by pilgrims after they have attended Mass at Downpatrick and then collected earth from Patrick's supposed grave. The wells are especially visited around midsummer and just before Lammas (August 1st) or Lughnasadh. At midnight between Midsummer's Eve and Midsummer's Day, a magical time when the veil between this world and the next is thin, the water rises and overflows in the largest of the wells. Pilgrims believe that the healing power of the wells is strongest at this time. (Logan 1980).

In Co. Donegal, a holy well dedicated to the saint can be found on the coast near the abbey of Ballysherman. It bubbles out of a hollow in the rocks and people hang rags on the bushes near it as offerings. A cave next to the well, possibly lived in by the guardian of the well in former times, is said to have been Patrick's private chapel. At another Patrick well in Co. Meath cattle were driven to it and sprinkled with water to bless them in a ritual dating back to pre-Christian times. In West Galway, local people gathered at a hilltop well dedicated to the saint on the last Sunday in July. This was said to be a folk memory of the old Lughnasadh celebrations.

Proof these holy wells were formerly pagan sites is given in M. O'Donnell's Life of Columcille (1918). The Irish saint Columcille, better known as Columba, visited a spring that was an ancient 'cursing well'. It was used by the druids and anyone who washed in it or drank the water was struck down with blindness or paralysis. The saint washed his hands in it without ill-effect and from then on it was a well known for its healing properties.

One of the most prominent female saints in Celtic Christianity was St Brigid, also known as Brigdhe, Bridget, Bride or Biddy. She was originally a Celtic goddess, possibly Brigantia, the 'High One' or 'Great Queen' worshipped by the Celtic tribe of the Brigantia. They were of Iberian origin and settled in northern and mid-Britain, including Northumbria, Cumbria, Lancashire and Yorkshire, Derbyshire, Nottingham, Cheshire and parts of North Wales. (Ragland Phillips 1976). As well as Brigantia this tribe worshipped a horned ram or bull god who the Romans identified with Silvanus, the god of the forest. To the Brigantians he was however a warrior god of fertility. (Ross 1967).

Brigantia or Brighde was a mother goddess of triple aspect and has been identified with St Brigid, who adopted much of her symbolism and attributes in the Christianisation process that followed pagan conversions. (Ross 1967). Brighde has a multiplicity of attributions and has variously been seen as a goddess of fire, the sun, the moon, animal husbandry, smithcraft, childbirth, the family, the hearth, midwifery, spinning and weaving, music, poetry, war, medicine, divination and, last but not least, fertility. She has rightly been called the archetypal Great Mother or 'Mother of the Gods' and combines all the aspects of the old pagan goddesses in one deity. (McCrickard 1987).

She has also been compared with The Mothers, the triad of Celtic goddesses, while the Romans identified her with Sulis-Minerva, the Romano-British goddess worshipped at Bath. Brigantia was also identified in Roman times with Minerva in her aspect as a war goddess. At Dumfrieshire in Scotland a relief portrays Brigantia with the symbols of Minerva. Caesar, in his description of the pagan beliefs of the Gauls, states they worship Minerva as a goddess of healing and thermal springs (Ross 1967). In Irish mythology, Brighde was the daughter of Dagda, the sky-father god of fertility and the goddess of the River Boyne. In Gaelic her name means 'fiery arrow', although McCrickard (1987) traces it back to the Sanskrit Brihati meaning 'the exalted one' and this also one of the title of Brigantia.

McCrickard also identifies Brighde with Sulis Minerva, pointing out that Sulis or Sul means 'eye' and is a symbolic reference to 'the eye of heaven' i.e. the sun. She further makes connections between Sul and Suale, the Baltic sun goddess, suggesting Brighde/Sulis Minerva was a version of the

Indo-European solar/fire goddess. In the myths of many other Indo-European peoples, including the Germans and the Scandinavians, the sun is represented as female. In Gaelic the word for sun is grian and this is a feminine form (McCrickard 1990).

In Celtic Christian hagiography, St Brigid is described as the daughter of a woman who was a slave owned by a druid called Dubthach or 'the dark one'. As a child the saint was fed milk by a faery cow with a white body and red ears. One day Brigid's mother left her alone while she went to tend the cows and when she looked back at the house was horrified to see it ablaze. She ran back to find it was not on fire but the light was shining from the baby's cradle.

At puberty, while still a virgin, Brigid decided to enter the Church and become a nun. In one version Patrick accidentally read the wrong words and ordained her as a priest. In other accounts she was even made an archbishop with the power to appoint the Irish bishops. These stories may be exaggerations to make her more important then she was or could reflect the power of women as pagan priestesses and the considerable influence of the female abbots in the Celtic Church who were known to act as priests.

The goddess Brighde was represented in triple form and this was also a feature of Brigid who is sometimes said to be three different women. These three Brigids were sisters and had dedicated their lives to various crafts and skills. One practised healing, another was a smith and the third was a poet and diviner. Collectively the three Brigids were known as The Mothers or The Three Blessed Ladies of Britain (McCrickard 1987).

Brigid's feast day was Imbolc or Candlemas at the beginning of February. In Gaelic Imbolc meant 'ewe's milk' and traditionally marked the beginning of lambing when the first signs of spring could be seen. For this reason, Brigid's sacred flower was the snowdrop, a symbol of regeneration and rebirth, and in Wales today country people still say the first snowdrop marks the end of winter. Imbolc, sometimes known in traditional witchcraft circles today as The Festival of Light, was dedicated to 'women's mysteries' and is a time of initiation and rebirth.

Imbolc has been described as a festival originating in the re-emergence of Brigid as a young virgin from the mountain wilderness. On a mystical level it is 'A festival sacred to the woman and the goddess of love..It is a time of initiation and beginnings..a transition towards becoming more independent again. An invocation of the life force and a renewal of its potency.' (Kindred 1991).

The cult of St Brigid centred on her church and abbey erected within a circular enclosure at Kildare or Kil Dara, 'the church of the oak.' Giraldus Cambrensis, who visited the site, said the nuns of Brigid looked after a 'perpetual flame' or fire that had to be tended in shifts day and night so it was never allowed to burn out. The shrine was allegedly surrounded by a wooden fence and no men were allowed to pass through this barrier. There were also separate entrances for men and women to the actual church and once inside the sexes were segregated. The sacred fire ritual continued from the time of Brigid, the beginning of the 6th century, until the early 13th century. It was then that the Archbishop of Dublin ruled the tending of the fire was a pagan practice and outlawed it. After the his death the practice was revived and continued until the Reformation.

Brigid seems to have left Kildare and travelled to other parts of the British Isles including Cornwall, Scotland and Wales. One of the places she visited was Glastonbury and she spent several years in meditation and prayer on the Isle of Beckery, a corruption of 'Little Ireland' from the Gaelic Beag Erin. A chapel already stood on the island dedicated to Mary Magdalene, but this was re-dedicated to Brigid in the 10th century. Two ancient representations of the saint survive in Glastonbury today. Both depict her milking a cow and can be seen in the Lady Chapel of Glastonbury Abbey and on the tower of St Michael's chapel on the Tor.

These illustrations are symbolic of Brigid's tradition association with fertility and fecundity. They also connect her with the faery cow of her birth and the popular legend she was the midwife to the Virgin Mary and foster-mother to Jesus. In Scotland, where she is known as Bride or Breed, a folk tale says Brigid baptised Jesus by sprinkling him with three drops of water on his forehead. This ritual was still carried out by Scottish midwives in rural districts until fairly recent times. R.J. Stewart says of this baptism rite; 'This tale is a Christianised rationalisation of an ancient Celtic myth, that of the birth of the son of Light, and the blessing of triple purity of the three drops of wisdom on his brow.' (1990)

There is another legend about Brigid saying that she wore a crown of lighted candles as a distraction to prevent Herod's troops from finding the baby Jesus during the Massacre of the Innocents. In the apocryphal Gospel of Thomas a spider weaves a web to protect Jesus at this time. This story link the massacre, in reality the sacrifice of the firstborn, with the ancient weaving goddess of fate, whose symbolic totem was a spider, and one of her aspects was Brighde.

Brigid/Brighde is also closely associated, as are all triple goddesses, with that aspect of the witch goddess known as the Faerie Queen or the Queen of Elfane, venerated by the medieval witch cult and modern traditional witches. A Gaelic folk ritual celebrated on Candlemas involved making a serpent, symbol of wisdom and the underworld, out of peat and placing it on the threshold of the house, a symbolic crossing-over point between the spirit world and Middle Earth. An incantation was chanted as follows: " This is the day of bride/ The Queen shall come out from the mound/I will not touch the Queen/The Queen will not touch me' This 'Queen' was the triple goddess of the underworld, death, spiritual transformation, initiation, sexuality and death. The 'mound' was the cromlech or burial chamber used for initiations and popularly regarded as entrances to the Otherworld or Faeryland.

Brigid was given almost equal status with the Virgin Mary in the Celtic Church. She was even given the title 'Queen of Heaven' that was usually only reserved for Our Lady. The saint's festival also coincided with Candlemas or the Purification of the Virgin (after childbirth). The Christian name for Imbolc came from the practice of blessing the candles to be used during the year on that day. Again there is the connection with light and fire and one more example of St Brigid's link with the ancient sun goddess of Europe.

Chapter Seven
Romans & Celts

While Patrick was busy fighting magical battles with druids and Brigid and her nuns were tending the perpetual fire at Kildare, the high king Vortigern was making his pact with the Saxons and the invasion of southern Britain had began. Arguments still rage among archaeologists and historians as to how the Saxonisation of the British took place.

Recently Dr Nicholas Higham of Manchester University expressed his opinion that the English are really descended from the Celts not the Saxons. He claims the Saxon 'invasion' was in fact a coup by a few thousand mercenaries who then imposed their culture downwards through society on to the Celtic population. Perhaps, if Highman is correct, we should be talking about Celto-Saxons or Saxon -Celts rather then Anglo-Saxons. Whether this theory is correct or not, the historical evidence offers a picture of a series of battles between the Celts and Saxons during the so-called Arthurian Age and the establishment of settled Saxon communities in southern England and as far north as Cumbria.

The Saxons were pagans when they arrived in Britain and therefore they posed not only a threat to the socio-political structure of the country but also to its (Christian) religious life. In what later became England - the Land of the Angles - Celtic Christian missions were launched by saints like Columba, Aidan and others in the 6th and 7th centuries to convert the Saxons in the north of the country and the pagan Picts in Scotland.

Although history books refer to the Saxons or Anglo-Saxons, the people who arrived here were a mixture of Saxons, Jutes and Angles from Germany, the Low Countries and the fringes of Scandanavia. They settled in southern England initially, giving their names to Essex (West Saxons), Sussex (South Saxons) and Wessex (West Saxons). Kent was occupied by the Jutish tribes and the Angles travelled north to East Anglia (East Angles) and north to Cumbria and Northumbria.

The pagan newcomers brought the worship of their own pantheon of gods. Their major deities were Woden, Thunor, Tiw and Frigga. Woden was the Germanic version of the Norse shaman god of the runes, Odin. He was also known as Grimr, 'the Masked One' or 'Hooded One', but his principal name came from the Indo-European Wodenaz. In Old High German he was known as Wuotan and this developed into the Saxon Wodan and finally into Old English Woden. In his original form he was a wind and storm god who ruled the dead and was leader of the Wild Hunt. The Saxon kings claimed that they were descended from Woden,who is sometimes regarded as having been a famous and mortal tribal chief or sacred king.

Tiw, Tew or Tiwaz, whose Norse equivalent was Tyr, was a sky god and is believed to have been the original creator god of Germanic mythology. Again he is a typically Indo-European deity and has strong mythic connections with the Greek god Zeus and the Roman gods, Jupiter and Mars. At some time, possibly at the beginning of the Christian era, Tiw lost his status as chief of the gods and was usurped by Woden (Branston 1974). Thunor was represented in the Norse myths by Thor, the god of thunder. In the Saxon myths he was the son of Woden and the Earth Mother and his symbol was the oak tree. When the Celts first encountered him they regarded him as the Roman Jupiter, a version of their own thunder god Taranis or Esus, the oak tree god. Frigga comes from the Indo-European Prij, meaning love, and she is depicted as the consort of Woden and the 'Mother of the Gods'. She is sometimes confused with the earth goddess Jorth and the medieval writer Snorri Sturlusson says she contains all aspects of the goddesses of northern Europe.

In addition to these deities, the Saxons worshipped another god borrowed from the Norse myths - Baldur. He was the young god of light and his Old English name, Baelder, translates as 'Lord'. He can be compared with the Middle Eastern vegetation /saviour gods such as Tammuz, Adonis, Baal, Attis and Mithras and is described as one of the consorts of 'Lady Earth'. His wyrd or fate is to die at the hands of a Judas-type figure, the fire god Loki. Although Baldur is banished to the underworld at Ragnorak, the end of the world, he is reborn to fight in the last struggle between the powers of darkness and light and eventually he rules the world.

Considering the Baldur myth it is not surprising that during the period of dual faith, when Christianity and paganism existed side by side, he was often identified with the Christ. Both Baldur and Odin/Woden were regarded as prototype Christ figures by the early Saxon converts to the new religion. This does not confirm the Christian propaganda that the Saxons willing, and eagerly, embraced Christianity and that within a short time paganism had been eradicated.

Even Branston (1974) appears to subscribe to this misconception when he says the Saxons arrived about 450 and were all converted by the middle of the 7th century. The evidence suggests the process took much longer and was more protracted then many historians would like us to believe. As we shall see the first Augustinian mission had to flee the country in the face of pagan threats and in the 7th century Rome was forced to send a second mission to prevent a pagan revival. The arrival of the pagan Vikings in the 9th and 10th centuries added to an already unpredictable situation.

The beginning of the end for the Celtic Church can be dated from the arrival of Augustine's mission in 597. Previous to his arrival there had been limited contact between the Celtic Church and Rome, although some of the Celtic saints had visited the Popes. Augustine's futile attempts to bring the Celtic Church in Britain under Roman authority is proof that the Celtic Christians regarded themselves as an independent body outside the rule of the Roman See. The practical reason for Pope Gregory wanting to despatch a mission to England had nothing to do with Angle slaves. In the world of real politics he wanted to save the souls of the Saxons heathens for Rome before the British (Celtic) Church could make missionary inroads into the areas they had occupied.

Mary-Harting (1972) is of the opinion that the Pope's intentions in launching the mission was to extend the power of the papacy and reform the wayward Gallic Church. In a letter written to the Bishop of Arles when the mission left Rome in July 597, the Pope asked that the Gallic church provide hospitality and support to Augustine and his monks as they pass through Gaul. In this same letter he informs the bishop that he is sending a papal emissary with the mission who will remain behind in Gaul and assist the Gallic church.

Gregory and Augustine deliberately chose Kent for the start of their enterprise as they knew King Ethelbert of the Jutes was sympathetic to the new religion, even though his subjects were pagans. His wife, Bertha or Berctha, was the grand-daughter of Clovis, the first Christian Merovingian king of the Franks. She had also been baptised and had her own personal Frankish chaplain with the rank of bishop. They worshipped at St Martin's church at Canterbury which dated from Roman times and was one of three churches Augustine restored after he arrived. The other two were being used for pagan worship and had to be reclaimed and reconsecrated.

The primary, and almost only, source of information on Augustine's mission is the Venerable Bede's Ecclesiastical History of the English Church and People, written in 731 .by the Catholic monk at a monastery in Jarrow. In Bede's account Augustine arrived on the Isle of Thanet in Kent and sought an audience with King Ethelbert. While he tolerated his wife's beliefs, the king was a superstitious man and at first believed the Christians might be practitioners of the magical arts. For this reason he only agreed to meet them outdoors as he believed the monk's alleged magical powers would be weakened in the open air.

Ethelbert at first was wary at accepting the new religion and abandoning his 'age-old beliefs'. However he did grant the mission permission to stay and preach in his kingdom and found them lodgings in Canterbury. At first Augustine used St Martin's for services and later, as some of the locals converted, Ethelbert gave permission for new churches to be built for the growing congregation. His reluctance to convert at this time, although it seems he did late, was due to the strength of the Old Religion in Kent at that time. Within a radius of twelve miles of Canterbury were five major sites used for heathen worship. (Mayr-Harting 1972).

In November 597 Augustine left England to visit Arles, where he was consecrated as the 'Archbishop of the English' by archbishop Etherius of the Gallic Church. Previously Augustine had only held the rank of an abbot. His consecration was part of the long-term Romanist plan to promote the authority of Rome over the Gauls and the Celtic Church in

Britain. Following his elevation to archbishop, Augustine returned to Canterbury full of missionary zeal. He began a new campaign to win converts and on Christmas Day 597 it is said 10,000 pagans were baptised in the River Medway.

The second Gregorian mission, led by Abbot Mellitus and including Paulinus who later restored the chapel at Glastonbury, carried with them the equipment and regalia needed to establish the Roman Church on a physical level. This included sacred vessels, altar coverings, priests' vestments, church ornaments and holy relics. As result of the second mission, twelve bishops were consecrated in southern England and they were administered by a bishop in London. A bishopric was also established in York to extend Roman Christianity northwards into the territory of the Celtic Church.

Mellitus also brought a letter to Augustine from the Pope. This famous document instructed the head of the mission not to destroy the Saxon pagan temples and sanctuaries. Instead, if these temples were well constructed, they should be sprinkled with holy water and have Christian altars set up in them. On the pagan festivals, when the blot or animal sacrifices took place, the people should be persuaded to still come to the former temples and kill the animals but they should use the meat to celebrate the saint's days with 'solemn feasting.'

In 598 there are signs Augustine was worried about the authority of his mission in England and, more importantly, his powers of jurisdiction, if any, over the existing British Church. He wrote to the Pope asking for advice on these matters and for instructions on how to deal with the Gallic bishops and the bishops of the Celtic Church in Britain. Gregory replied and told Augustine that he gave him no powers over the Gauls. In respect of the British he said: 'We trust you, brother, that the unlearned may be taught, the weak strengthened by persuasion, the perverse to be corrected by authority.' (Wade-Evans 1934).

In 602 or 603 Augustine decided to meet with the bishops and spiritual leaders 'of the nearest British province'. This meeting took place near the Severn on the Welsh Border between lands held by the Hwicca tribe and the West Saxons. Significantly the gathering was held under an ancient oak tree that became known after the event as Augustine's Oak. We know both the druids and the Saxons venerated the oak and this special significance was taken up by the Church. The early missionaries often preached under ancient oaks previously used for pre-Christian ceremonies and these became known as 'Gospel Oaks'. One famous example stands at the bottom of Parliament Hill in London. In Celtic times this hill was called Llandin and was a druidic centre. After his coronation Edward the Confessor received the charter of rights for the citizens of London seated under this tree.

At this meeting under the sacred oak Augustine suggested to the British bishops that the Celtic and Roman Churches should unite and they should join his crusade to convert the pagans. In his description of this meeting Bede notes that the Celts did not keep 'the correct date' for Easter and 'certain of their customs were at variance with the universal practice of the (Roman) Church'. In fact the Celtic Church differed significantly from the Roman rule in several important matters of theology and practice. For this reason the discussions soon broke down, because the British were not willing to give up their prisci mores, or ancient customs. They told the new archbishop of the Roman Church in England that they could not contemplate this action without the consent of their followers.

The main difference cited by Bede was the dating of Easter. This festival is the most important one in the Christian calendar and the Romanists believed all Christians should celebrate it at the same time. Between the 2nd and 6th centuries different methods were used to calculate the date of Easter. The Council of Arles in 314 ruled Easter should be observed on the same day by everyone. In 325 the Council of Nicea ruled that it should always be celebrated on a Sunday.

The Council of Orleans in 541 agreed a formula for calculating the date based on the full moon nearest to the vernal equinox. This method was similar to the method used by the Jews to calculate their Paschal or Passover festival which coincided with Easter. This system was agreed by the Roman Church but not by their Celtic brethren. Instead the Celtic Church followed a dating method recommended by Pope Leo in 453. This was based on a lunar cycle of eighty four years and was possibly connected with the old Celtic lunar calendar.

The liturgy and practices of the Celtic Church also differed from the Roman. To add to the problem the Welsh Church also differed from the Gallic, Scottish and Irish Churches, which all had their own slightly different ways of worship and procedure. If Roman Catholicism was to become the universally accepted and orthodox version of Christianity throughout Europe, and that was the Vatican's grand plan, then these differences had to be eliminated and all the Churches had to be brought into line under the Roman rule.

The major differences, apart from the 'wrong' date for Easter, were in the rites of ordination, with the Welsh Church for instance practising several unique rituals. These included the consecration of bishops by one bishop not two, the anointing of the head as well as the hands of the new priest, or in the case of a bishop the head twice, the prayer of giving the stole to a deacon, the rite of giving a copy of the Gospels to a deacon and the rite of investing a priest with a stole. These differences may not seem important to a layperson but the rituals of ordination were an essential ceremony of the Church because they passed on the apostolic succession from the Pope as the Vicar of Christ.

The Celtic Church also practised triple immersion at baptisms and an unusual healing rite based on washing the feet of the sick person. Bishops wore crowns instead of mitres and the Mass was often carried out by two priests. Celtic priests and monks also wore a different tonsure to their Roman brethren. The clergy of Rome shaved the crown of their heads, leaving a fringe or circle of hair, representing the crown of thorns. The Celtic clergy shaved the front of their heads in a style worn by the druids. hence the Romanists thought the Celtic tonsure was 'heretical'.

One of the reasons why the so-called 'druidic tonsure' was regarded as heretical was because it was the hairstyle adopted by Simon Magus in the 1st century. He is described by clerical writers as a 'magician' and 'wonder worker' and is sometimes identified with the Anti-Christ. In fact the cult that grew up around him became a serious challenge to Christianity at one time. Simon Magus had a female disciple called Helen who was allegedly the representative on Earth of the goddess Sophia or Wisdom, the Shekinah of the Jewish Cabbala.

As Alby Stone has pointed out, hair length and the rules to regulate it were a serious matter in the early Church. Long hair was associated with the survival of pagan beliefs and homosexuality, while short hair was regarded as 'manly' and a sign of good Christian character and morality. In pre-Christian times there seems to have been a tradition of ritual hairstyles with religious significance and the folklore associated with this survived into the Middle Ages. (Stone 1992)

Other differences seem to have centred on the influence of Judaism on Celtic Christianity. We may speculate this influence may have come from Joseph of Arimathea, who was a Nazarene. Apart from the link between Easter and the Passover, originally the Celts celebrated the Sabbath on a Saturday in the Judaic manner rather then on Sunday. After a lot of discussion the days were changed over but the Jewish belief that no work should be done on the Sabbath survived. It is only in the last twenty years that public houses have been allowed to open in Wales on a Sunday, and while this may be the influence of the Methodist revival of the 1900s it is in accordance with old Celtic Christian practices keeping the Sabbath as a holy day.

There was also the question of the philosophy behind the Celtic Church. The lives of the saints provide many examples of the subtle, and not so subtle way, early Celtic Christianity was influenced and permeated by earlier spiritual beliefs and practices. The Celtic Church's attitude to women, while reflecting the general misogyny of Christianity, was quite liberal compared with Catholicism. In pre-Christian times Celtic women had a higher social status then in the Middle Ages. As McCrickard says: ' A Celtic tribe was equally as likely to be ruled by a queen as a king, the women were not regarded as weaker, deficient or inept in any way.' (1987). The Goddess figure played an important symbolic role in Celtic Christianity and 'The Celtic Church was an independent form of Christianity which in part had derived its view of women from the pagan past - here, though within a patriarchal society, women had great freedom, dignity and temporal and spiritual power'.

In the Celtic Church female abbots performed priestly duties and we saw how St Brigid was allegedly ordained as a priest and even became an archbishop. By the 9th century the Roman Church was attempting to remove the powers of these Celtic women priests. In 816 the Synod of

Aix-la Chapelle outlawed the right of women abbots to practice as priests or initiate nuns. Eight years later the Synod of Paris issued an edict banning women from giving communion or serving at the altar during Mass.

On a theological level it has been suggested Celtic Christianity was influenced by the Arian heresy which rejected the concept of the Trinity. (Hardinge 1972). This heresy had been founded in 4th century Alexandria and was outlawed at Nicea in 325. The so-called Nicean Creed taught that God and Jesus were one and the same and it prohibited the alternative idea that Jesus was just a mortal man or the Gnostic idea that he was a special human being who had been overshadowed by the Christ. The Celtic baptismal ceremony omitted any reference to the Trinity and St Columba was reprimanded by the Pope for not stressing belief in the 'three persons' of God.. The general Celtic Christian attitude to God seems to have been the esoteric view; that little was known about the mysteries of Divinity and human speculation about its nature was pointless. There is also a broad hint that the Celtic Church did not believe Jesus really was the 'Son of God' and instead was preaching the existence of an all-powerful Godhead and a human Jesus. (Starbird 1993).

Celtic Christianity also received its mystical inspiration from the Gospel of St John the Divine or Revelations. In Christian tradition, and especially Esoteric Christian tradition, this gospel has been regarded as a mystical one because it describes the cosmic events preceding Armageddon, the end of the world, and the Second Coming. It also describes the creation of the New Jerusalem and this vision has been connected with Joseph of Arimathea and the first native British church established by him at Glastonbury. (Michell 1973 & 1983)

An esoteric tradition exists that St John may have bee a Celt. This idea was first publicly aired in a paper given to the Scottish lodge of the Theosophical Society in 1894. It links with the legend of Paul's alleged visit to Britain and the, rather fanciful, theory that the British, more specifically the Welsh, were descendants of one of the lost tribes of Israel. Pictures of John found in the catacombs are offered as proof that physically the saint was fair-haired Celt and not a dark-haired Semite like some of the other disciples. (Hartley 1968).

All these differences in ritual and doctrine would have been raised and discussed at the meeting between Augustine and the British bishops. Bede reports Augustine brought the sterile discussions to a halt by calling on God to send a sign from Heaven. This would show the assembly the right tradition to follow. A blind man then wandered into the gathering and Augustine challenged the Celtic clergy to heal him. When they tried and failed, Augustine knelt and prayed and the man's sight was restored.

In Bede's account, the British bishops were awed at this miracle and recognised Augustine as 'the herald of the light of Christ'. They also, Bede says, accepted the doctrines he taught as 'the way of righteousness'. However, they also insisted that the ancient customs of their Church could not be abandoned without consulting their congregation. They therefore asked for a second meeting to be convened following this consultation and Augustine agreed.

The Celtic clergy may or may not have been impressed by Augustine's miracle, which reads like the type of wonder-working practised by the saints to impress the pagans, but before the second meeting they took the precaution of consulting a holy man for advice. They asked the sage if they should trust the Roman missionary and abandon their Celtic ways as he demanded. In reply the holy man said if Augustine was truly a man of God then they should follow him and do as he said. When the bishops asked how they could tell, the holy man said the test was whether he would receive them in a haughty or arrogant manner or be meek and lowly. If he rose from his chair to greet them he was a genuine servant of Christ, but if he remained seated they should not trust him.

The second meeting duly took place near Chester on the Welsh Border and was attended by seven bishops and '..many men of learning' (Wade-Evans 1934). The latter were mostly from the monastic centre at Bangor on the River Dee in North Wales. When the Celtic clergy approached Augustine remained seated and, in what appears to have been a deliberate snub, refused to greet them. The British clergy became angry at this show of arrogance and bad manners. They accused the archbishop of the sin of pride and he counter-attacked by criticising them for not observing the Catholic (universal) rule.

Augustine said he would accept some of their customs, except for the different dating of Easter. He insisted they accept the Roman form of baptism and the tonsure and joined with him in a crusade to convert the heathens. The British refused to accept his demands and told him plainly that neither did they accept his authority over their Church. By this action they effectively challenged the apostolic authority claimed by the Pope. Incensed at their refusal to conform, Augustine issued a veiled warning that, Bede infers, was also a prophecy. He said if the British clergy refused to accept peace with their fellow Christians, then they would be forced to accept war at the hands of their enemies.

This prophecy allegedly came to pass when Ethelfrith, the Saxon king of Northumbria, swept down and attacked the Welsh at Chester in 617. Before the battle the king spied a large gathering of monks and priests on the enemy side praying for victory over the English. He ordered his men to attack them and over a thousand, many from Bangor and some who attended the second meeting with Augustine, were killed. This event was recorded by Irish chroniclers as 'the Slaughter of the Saints'.

The second meeting between Augustine and the British bishops seems to have been the last attempt for sixty years to convert the Celtic Church to Catholicism Augustine died in 604 an in 610 Bishop Dagon of Inverdaoile was authorised by the Irish Celtic Church to visit Canterbury and meet with the new Archbishop Laurentius. His brief was to discuss the differences between the two Churches and possibly agree to a reconciliation.

It seems to have been a stormy and unproductive meeting with the Romanists complaining that the bishop would not eat with them, or even have a meal in the same house, Dagon was apparently upset by the arrogant attitude of the foreign missionaries and walked out of the talks. He accused them of coming to Britain without having gained any prior knowledge of Celtic culture and of treating the British clergy as heretics because they followed different customs.

Laurentius wanted unity between the Celtic and Roman Churches, but on his terms. He also wanted to extend the Gregorian mission to the Picts and Gaels. The stumbling block was the Celtic Church who he regarded as 'unorthodox'. Nearly sixty years later another Archbishop of

Canterbury would go one further an denounce the Celtic persuasion as heretical. Laurentius however had his one problems as well. With the death of Augustine the mission he led seems to have faltered and the danger of failure became a real possibility.

When King Ethelbert died in 616, his son Eadbald reverted to paganism. Bede paints a sensational portrait of Eadbald as an insane fornicator who married his father's second wife and was possessed by evil spirits. Eadbald's pagan revival was supported by the sons of the recently deceased king of the East Saxons in Essex. They had been converted but after their father's death they encouraged their people to go back to the worship of the Old Gods. When they saw Bishop Mellitus offering Mass in a local church they demanded that the eucharist should be given to them. When the bishop refused because they had abandoned the Church for the pagan ways, the sons drove him into exile with all his followers.

Faced with this humiliating defeat, Mellitus returned to Canterbury and consulted with his fellow bishops. It was decided that under the present conditions it would be safer if the mission withdrew from England rather then remain without power among a pagan people. Mellitus decamped to Gaul but Bede says a Bishop Laurence (Laurentius?) remained in Kent. One night St Peter materialised in his room and threatened him with a scourge. He told the bishop he should stay and reconvert the pagans and the saint offered his own life as an example of suffering for the Christian faith.

The next morning Laurence sought an audience with King Eadbald and told him about the visitation from St Peter. He removed his robe and showed the pagan king the lash marks on his back. Bede says, Eadbald was so impressed by the story that he renounced his idolatry, accepted baptism and began to promote the Christian faith among his people. He also sent a message to Mellitus in Gaul inviting him and the other bishops to return in safety. When they did most of the people welcomed them back, except the Londoners who refused to accept Mellitus as their bishop and still put their faith in their pagan priests.

It is clear that the Gregorian missions were not the success history teaches us they were. Even where Christianity had been accept the old beliefs lived on by its side. King Redwald, another ruler of the East Saxons, for instance had a pagan wife and in the church he attended there were two altars. One for Christian use and the other to worship the pagan gods. Such practices of dual faith continued for many years. When Christianity did eventually gain the upper hand, the Old Ways were merely driven underground and re-emerged in other forms such as witchcraft.

During the sixty year period between the death of Augustine and the Synod of Whitby in 664, the Roman Church battled against the tide of paganism in the areas it had converted. Roman Christianity was slowly established in East Anglia, Wessex, Sussex, the Midlands and those regions in the north of England not already under Celtic Christian influence. The Romanists were gradually establishing their own power structure, even though it was being strongly resisted by the Celtic Church and the revived paganism.

In 669 a third papal mission was sent to Britain in an attempt to prevent the complete collapse of Roman Christian beliefs in the country at that time. Archbishop Deusdedit of Canterbury had died in 664 and it took the Pope nearly five years to appoint his successor. Two Christian kings, Egbert and Oswy, in desperation sent their own candidate to Rome to be consecrated. Unfortunately he died of the plague that was sweeping Europe before he could return and take up his office.

Finally, in 669, the Pope appointed an elderly monk called Theodore of Tarsus in Asia Minor to be the new Archbishop of the English. He travelled to England with his companion Abbot Hadrian, who is described as an African, leading the third mission to combat paganism. He was more effective then the previous missions and, Bede says, quickly established the Roman rule. He laid down a series of regulations covering everything from the observance of Easter to the relationship of bishops with their parent houses and, most importantly, he passed legislation outlawing the survival of pagan practices. These laws against paganism specifically outlawed the wearing of ritual animal costumes, especially representing stags, at the midwinter celebrations. The casting of 'evil spells' was punished by seven years penance of fasting and prayer. Anyone caught practising 'devilish witchcraft' or divination was forced to serve a year's penance on bread and water.

Theodore also issued decrees dealing with the difficult relationship between the Roman and Celtic Churches. He declared 'Those ordained by Scottish or British (i.e. Welsh) bishops, who are not Catholics in the keeping of Easter and in the manner of the tonsure are not united to the (Roman) Church but must be confirmed by a Catholic bishop.' (Moorman 1953). Theodore also declared baptisms performed by Celtic clerics as invalid and any Catholic who attended a Celtic Mass was forced to do penance for a year - the same punishment as for practising witchcraft!

By such decrees the Roman Church sought to establish its spiritual monopoly. Effectively its plan was to destroy the influence and power of the old Celtic Church in the British Isles. Over the next five hundred it finally achieved its goal. The beginning of this process was the Council of Whitby and we shall examine this important event in the history of Celtic Christianity, and the Celtic missions to the pagan Picts, in the next chapter.

Chapter Eight
The Druid and the Monk

In the period when the first and second Gregorian missions were trying to establish a foothold in south-east England, in the north of the country Irish monks, who were later to became important saints in the Celtic Church, were busy bringing Christianity to the pagan Picts and Saxons in the region. The Picti or Picts were a mysterious race surrounded with myth, magic and mystery. They were called the Painted People by the Romans because of their body decoration. of ritual tattoos with a religious significance. The Romans (typically) regarded the Picts as savage barbarians, probably because they had little success in their campaigns north of the English border with Scotland. In fact they soon abandoned the idea of conquering Scotland and instead built first an earthwork then a stone wall to keep the Picts and other northern tribes out. When the Roman legions left the Picts breached the abandoned defences and invaded the country as far south as Wales.

The Celtic Church in Scotland and the Borders was established following several missions by Irish monks. Some of these would have belonged to the Order of Celi De, the Culdees, who were regarded, as we saw earlier as secret adherents of the Old Religion. Culdee settlements were often built on old druidic sites and St Bernard described the Irish Culdees as 'Christian in name, but in reality pagans' (Spence 1928). In practice the Culdees followed a strict and ascetic rule within the Celtic Church. Extreme sect members even preached against what they saw as the corruption and evil in the 'Old Church'. This militant tendency were totally opposed to the 'temptations of the flesh' and regarded women as 'devils incarnate'. However some Culdees must have married because the order had a hereditary priesthood in the druidic manner.

In 813 the Roman Church declared the Culdees to be heretics and three years later they were forbidden to officiate as priests. Culdee communities still survived after this edict as there were Culdee priests at St Peter's in York as late as 936. At the Priory of St Andrews in Fife, the Culdees continued to practise until the 12th century, celebrating Mass in a separate chapel from the Roman priests. (Hartley 1968).

Two of the prominent missionaries associated with the Church's early attempt to convert the Scoti and the Picts were SS Ninian and Kentigern. Ninian was the son of a 5th century Christian king on the Scottish border and as a young man was sent on a pilgrimage to Rome. He studied in a theological college there and became friendly with the Pope. As a result he was made a bishop and sent back to north-west Britain as a missionary. In those times, according to Ailred's The Life of St Ninian, the inhabitants of that region had either not heard of Christianity or had received the gospel from 'heretics or men ill-instructed in the law of God.' If Ailred can be believed, Ninian was received with open arms and built a church dedicated to St Martin of Tours, who he had met on his way back from Rome.

One of Ninian's first converts was a local king called Tuduvallis. At first he was opposed to the saint but his hatred of Christianity caused his kingdom to become a wasteland . Only thorns and thistles would grow there and even the king fell sick and withered. His sickness got worse and worse until he lost his sight and was unable to get out of bed. In desperation, Tuduvallis summoned Ninian and begged for healing. The saint placed his hands on the king's head and he was cured The ruler was so grateful he immediately converted and the wasteland flowered again.

Heartened by this success, Ninian launched a mission to convert the Picts who still worshipped 'deaf and dumb idols'. It is said he converted them by healing the sick, restoring the sight of the blind and even raising the dead. The Picts saw these miracles and 'renounced Satan', destroyed their pagan temples and idols and built churches to replace them.

Although the chronicler gives the impression Ninian was successful and Christianity became widespread in north -west Britain and southern Scotland as a result of his mission, in historical fact it was not until the late 6th and early 7th centuries that SS Columba and Kentigern had more success in converting the Picts, Celtic Britons and Saxons of northern Britain.

St Kentigern was of royal birth and his mother was a pagan princess who had converted but practised secretly in case her pagan father discovered. In the hagiography of Kentigern it is suggested his mother dedicated her life to the Virgin Mary and his birth was the result of an immaculate conception. One medieval chronicler has a more jaundiced view, and suggests the young woman may have been under the spell of a soothsayer or befuddled with alcohol when the event took place.

When the king found out about the pregnancy he refused to accept the idea of a virgin birth and demanded to know who the father was. His daughter insisted under oath she had not been with any man. Under the laws at the time any woman found guilty of fornication (i.e. sex outside marriage) in her father's house could be punished by being thrown from a high summit. Ninian's mother was sentenced to this punishment but when she was thrown from a nearby mountain she called on the Virgin and floated gently to earth like a feather. Some praised this as a miracle while others said she was sorceress who had used her magical arts to save herself from harm.

The king, who was 'devoted to idolatry', accepted the words of his pagan kinsfolk. He placed his daughter in a boat and set it adrift at sea. However, the boat was guided through the waves, as if by a powerful hand, and was washed up on the shore. Where it landed was near a Christian community led by an ex-druid called Servanus who taught young boys in the arts of priesthood. When the boat reached the land a choir of angels were heard singing and local shepherds were drawn by a light to find the princess and her new born baby.

Kentigern was raised as a monk at the community, although the other boys resented his fast progress and plotted to discredit him. One day they were playing with Servanus' pet robin and accidentally killed it. The boys blamed Kentigern but he outwitted them by replacing the bird's severed head and praying over it until it was restored to life. The bird flew off to greet its master on his return from Mass. Kentigern later raised the abbey's cook from the grave and those locals who witnessed this miracle instantly converted.

After many years of learning, Kentigern left the abbey to preach to the pagans. A king of the Cumbrian region appointed him as bishop to re-establish the Church and he was anointed by the Celtic Rite at the age of twenty five. He established his spiritual centre at Glasgu (Glasgow) and went about overthrowing 'the shrines of demons', casting down graven images and building new churches. He had an uncanny power over animals and once yoked a stag to a plough. That year the land was the most fertile it had ever been and there was a bumper harvest.

Not all the pagans accepted Kentigern and his message willingly. A king called Morken slandered the saint and said his famous miracles were magical illusions. In response Kentigern visited the king and asked for food for his monks. At first the king refused and then told the saint if he could transfer all the grain from his barns to the monastery he would feed the monks in the future. Kentigern caused the nearby river to flood and rise and it swept the king's barns to the monastery without getting a grain wet.

The king denounced Kentigern as a sorcerer and was joined in the attack by his counsellor - probably a druid or shaman- who knocked the saint to the ground. As the druid was leaving, his horse stumbled and he fell and broke his neck. Shortly afterwards the king's feet began to swell up and he died. People whispered the two deaths were the vengeance of the Christian god and, in fear, many converted.

Resistance to Kentigern did not end with the death of the king and his druid. A group of conspirators, described as 'sons of Belial' (pagans) plotted revenge and planned to assassinate the saint. Fearing attack Kentigern fled to Wales and sought refuge at Mynyw or St David's. On his journey he stopped at the old Roman city of Caerleon on the Welsh Border, where he heard that the hill tribes still worshipped 'false gods'. He preached to them and many were converted. While at Mynyw Kentigern was granted land by a local tribal king to build a monastery. He was led to the building site by a wild boar from the nearby woods. Unfortunately the local tribes resented his presence and a pagan prince called Melconde Galgaru ordered his warriors to attack the saint's temporary camp. On his way home the prince was struck blind. He was taken back to the saint who healed him and the prince was baptised and ordered his men to help Kentigern build his monastery in peace.

The hagiography of Kentigern says after he fled south his homeland was ravaged by plague and famine. Many of his new converts reverted to the Old Ways, the crops failed and the cattle died. A king then took the throne who had been baptised in Ireland and he invited Kentigern back to preach the gospel. At first the saint was reluctant to return until an angel told him in a dream he must go north and establish a 'holy nation'. On his return Kentigern showed the people that their pagan gods were 'dumb, vain inventions of men, fitter for the fire then worship'.

He also said the elemental forces they worshipped as deities were the creations of God provided to help humankind. He claimed Woden, their chief god, was a mortal man, a pagan king of the Saxons from whom many nations were descended but who now roasted in hellfire. Hearing this explanation the people readily converted. Kentigern prayed to God to lift the curse on the land and it began to rain. Green shoots sprung up from the barren earth and even the queen, who was sterile, conceived. The king was overjoyed and begged Kentigern on his knees to take his throne and rule over the land.

Kentigern's death was surrounded by mysterious omens, strange portents and bizarre events. The saint had decided his work was complete and he wanted to die so he prepared himself to leave his body. As his followers prayed at his bedside an angel materialised and said that if any of them wanted to join the saint in Heaven the next day they should follow his instructions. The next day a bath was filled with warm water and the saint was placed in it. He closed his eyes and died. Those of his disciples who wanted to follow him then took turns to step into the bath and as soon as they laid down they also died

The religious situation during the 6th century when SS Columba and Aidan carried out their missions to the pagan north lands was confused. Sixty years before the coming of Augustine, St Columba or Colmcille had crossed over from Ireland at the invitation of King Conall of Argyll and settled with one hundred and fifty monks and priests on the Isle of Hy, Ishona or Iona. This island had been a druidic stronghold and in Gaelic was known as Inis Druineach or 'Druid's Isle'. (Hardinge 1972).

When he arrived on the island Columba found that another missionary called Oran had arrived some years before him and set up a monastery dedicated to St John the Divine. He also found two 'bishops' in residence who were either Culdees or disguised druids and they disputed his right to be there (Hartley 1968). The saint also seems to have had some problems with druids in Ireland. He had founded a monastery at a place called Dearmach, the Gaelic for 'field of oaks', and this name suggests it was previously a druidic sacred grove.

The archdruid on Iona, Gwendollau, was Welsh and when the saint he arrived he complained to his fellow druid, Myrddin (surely not Merlin of Arthurian legend?), that he could no longer practise his rites in the 'raised circles' because the 'grey stones' had been removed, presumably by the monks. (Hartley 1968). This is an interesting example of the druidical use of the stone circles for rituals as late as the 6th century. Iona was also the resting place of the druids' so-called 'Black Stone of Destiny'. Hartley identifies this sacred object with the Lia Fail of Irish myth and says Columba crowned King Aedan on it. It was later taken to Scone, where it was used to crown the Scottish monarchs, and it resides today in Westminster Abbey as the Coronation Stone. (1968).

Despite the opposition of the druids, Columba stayed on Iona and once established launched several missions on to the mainland. He also became the spiritual advisor to King Aeldan, who was of Irish descent and had extended his realm from parts of Ireland, to the Isle of Man and the Orkneys. He had also become Lord of the Picts and had marched south to do battle with the Angles. It is said that Columba participated in some of these battles, fighting hand-to-hand alongside the king as on of his personal bodyguard of warriors.

The saint's primary duty was to act as a spiritual advisor to the king. In this respect he was taking the old role of the druids who, in this position, were called 'soul friends'. It was an hereditary title and, as most druids were married, was passed to their eldest sons. In Celtic Christianity women often played this role and it was often a position granted to foster-mothers. They were regarded as 'spiritual mothers' who could hear confessions and may be connected with the 'faery godmothers' of folklore. (Hardinge 1972). It is not very speculative to see in these women's roles memories of the priestesses and wise women of the Old Faith.

Columba appears to have inherited the magical powers of the druids as well. He healed the sick, raised the dead, conducted magical battles with the pagans, fought demons, exorcised evil spirits and defeated supernatural monsters. The saint also had the power to control elemental forces and in one incident calmed a storm created by the druids to stop him returning to Iona. He owned a special white stone (a crystal?) which he used for healing. This he had found this in a river and blessed for his use. Such stones were used for similar purposes by the druids and were also used by Welsh witches in historical times.

One of the most interesting powers Columba possessed was his gift of prophecy and he had a famous reputation as a seer. His psychic powers included prediction, clairvoyance and extra-sensory perception. In common with most other Celtic saints, Columba could also see angels and experienced visions of the Otherworld. The saint predicted victory for his king in battle and on a visit to a monastery 'felt' a boy standing behind him. Although this child was despised by the monks, Columba predicted he would be a great cleric one day and this prediction came true. He also predicted that the dispute over the date of Easter would lead to the end of the Celtic Church and on another visit to a monastery he denounced the priest saying Mass as a secret criminal. He was forced to confess his sin to an astonished congregation. (Anderson 1961).

Columba also used his psychic powers to track down a man who was killing seals on Iona belonging to the monastery. Following the saint's instructions, the monks went to the hiding place he had indicated and found the man with a boat full of dead seals. Columba forgave the man and provided him with provisions so that he did not need to kill the seals. He also had a premonition of the man's death and sent a monk with a final gift of food. When he arrived he found the man had died

Seership, or the power of the Second Sight,. was well-known in Scotland and Columba's use of these gifts is part of an ancient tradition passed down from the druids to the Christian priesthood and the village wise women and cunning men. The most famous example of one of the Christian priests who inherited this art of seership was Robert Kirk. He was a 17th century Scottish clergyman who claimed to be able to see faeries, elemental spirits and visions of the Otherworld. R.J.Stewart suggests Kirk's book The Secret Commonweath may contain material describing a surviving cult of the Celtic goddess Brighde in Scotland (Stewart 1990). It is obvious from the book that Kirk met seers in the Highlands who were still following a hereditary Celtic, or even pre-Celtic, tradition. This esoteric tradition was enshrined in folklore, the belief in faeries and nature spirits, the power of the Second Sight and the curious practices of traditional witchcraft.

One of the strangest stories in Columba's hagiography is his close encounter with the Loch Ness 'monster'. While he was living in the land of the Picts the saint had to cross Loch Nesa (Ness). When he reached its banks he found some local people burying the body of a man who had been swimming in the loch and had been killed by the creature who dwelt in its dark, deep waters. Columba commanded one of his monks to swim across the narrowest part of the loch and retrieve a boat from the other side. Half way across Nessie appeared and attempted to attack the monk. The saint raised his hand in blessing and made the sign of the cross. The creature turned and fled leaving the monk to swim on in peace. The locals were so surprised at this that they converted.

One of the other prominent northern British saints was Aidan. He was also Irish and as a young boy in 577 he left to study with St David in West Wales and on the Isle of Iona. Aidan was invited by the Saxon king Oswald of Northumbria to convert the heathens in his kingdom. Oswald was later granted sainthood and is known in the Celtic Church as a 'king, saint and martyr'. He gave Aidan the island of Lindisfarne as his headquarters and the saint built a famous monastery there. Between them Oswald and Aidan were responsible for converting large numbers of pagans in Northumbria and the north of England.

When Oswald and Aidan visited a place later called Kirkoswald, literally 'the church of Oswald', they found the natives worshipping a stream of water flowing from a spring at the bottom of a hill. The saint and the king joined forces and built a church over this site. the locals converted, adopted Oswald as their patron saint and renamed the village after him. (Ragland Phillips 1976).

Oswald was killed in battle at Oswestry, Shropshire in 642 by King Penda of Mercia and after his death his body was mutilated in pagan fashion (Hunter Blair 1976). Bede describes Penda as a 'heathen king' and 'idol worshipper'. Like most of the Saxon kings, including Oswald before his conversion, Penda claimed descent from Woden. Bede does concede that Penda did not prohibit the preaching of Christianity to his subjects. What he did despise was anyone who was not sincere in their Christian faith once they had adopted it.

A cult of saintship, with pagan overtones, quickly grew up around Oswald. The patch of ground where he fell in battle and which was soaked in his blood was said to have stayed fresh and green while all the rest of the area was trampled down and brown. An admirer took some earth from the site and wrapped it in a linen cloth. While he was staying in lodgings the house burnt down but the earth, cloth and the beam it was on survived untouched. An unearthly light shone over Oswald's body as it lay in a wagon awaiting burial. People reported seeing a pillar of light shining up from the vehicle during the night. The water Oswald's bones were washed in was poured on the ground and the earth from the site was used for healing and exorcising evil spirits.

Penda had previously killed the Christian King Edwin in 633. He had united with the Celtic king Cadwalla and they had achieved many victories which, the 5th century Nennuis says, was because Penda had used 'the arts of the Devil, as he had never been baptised and never believed in God.' Because of Penda's campaign Bishop Paulinus of York, one of Augustine's missionaries, was forced to flee the city and took refuge in Kent where he was appointed as the bishop of Rochester. It was only later that Aidan and his monks recovered northern England for Celtic Christianity and extended their mission as far south as East Anglia.

Dr Margaret Murray claimed Penda as one of the early medieval 'divine kings', although other historians have cast doubt, with some justification, on her theories. Recently Alby Stone has noted that the dismemberment of Oswald's body, 'in the pagan fashion', by Penda and the reburial of parts of it all over the country accords with ancient sacrificial traditions. Penda was also responsible for the deaths of four other kings - Sigbert, Edwin, Anna and Edrith. When Penda was slain in battle himself in 655 'the earth was watered with his blood'. (Stone 1993).

Aidan died in 651 and after the death of his father, King Penda of Mercia accepted Christianity, but only after he was told by King Oswy that he could not marry his daughter unless he converted! In 653 the East Saxons accepted Christianity after a long pagan relapse. Oswy persuaded them that their gods were only 'logs of wood and blocks of stone'. The conversion of the East Saxons was carried out by St Cedd of Lindisfarne. He was one of the famous 'four brothers of Lindisfarne' and helped his other brother, Chad, convert the Mercians. The new Archbishop of Canterbury, Theodore the Greek, accused Chad of being ordained as a bishop by the 'irregular rites ' of the Celtic persuasion and he resigned his office and was reconsecrated by the Roman rule. (Hardinge 1972).

In 664 the theological conflict between the two Churches came to a head at the famous Council or Synod held at the monastery of Whitby. It was convened because of the chaos being caused by the conflicting doctrines and practices of the Celtic and Roman rule. In 634 and 640 Pope Honorius and Pope John had written to the Scottish Church about their 'error' in observing Easter and about the Pelagian heresy, which had been reived again in the north. The primary impetus for Whitby however seems to have come from King Oswy, whose wife was a Roman Christian This meant his court celebrated two Easters. The king therefore asked for the synod to be called to resolve the question once and for all.

It opened with St Cedd acting as an interpreter between the representatives of the Scottish Church and the Roma Church, because he spoke Latin, Old English and Gaelic. King Oswy started the discussion by observing that all who served God should follow the same rule. His bishop, Colman, then explained to the assembly that the customs of the Celtic Church were very ancient and could be traced back to St John the Divine. This was contested by a Romanist supporter, Wilfred, who pointed out that the early Church (the Nazarenes) followed Jewish practices and he referred to the words of St Peter about Easter and the earlier rulings of Nicea. He concluded arrogantly: " The only people who stupidly contend against the whole world are these Scots and their partners in obstinacy, the Picts and Britons, who inhabit only a portion of these the two uttermost islands of the oceans."

Winifred's diatribe seems to have won the argument. Colman reluctantly backed down and the Synod accepted the Roman date for Easter, allegedly given by Peter, and decreed it should be universally observed. Colman was unable to agree with this decision and he and his monks, and some of the Scottish clergy, returned to his homeland of Ireland where they could still practice in the Celtic way. A Roman Catholic bishop of Northumbria was appointed to replace him.

Following Whitby, the Roman dating of Easter and the Roman style tonsure were not automatically accepted by the other branches of the Celtic Church. In 709 Aldhelm, the bishop of Malmesbury, complained that the Welsh 'heretics' refused to pray with the Roman brethren. They even purified the utensils used by the Roman clergy with sand, and fire before they would eat off them and would not sit at the same table. In fact South Wales did not accept the Roman rule until 768 and in North Wales it was as late as 777. Bitterness and ill-feeling lasted a lot longer.

In 684 King Ecgfrid of Northumbria, a Roman Christian, invaded Northern Ireland in an attempt to destroy the Celtic Church. The Anglo-Saxon Chronicle describes the event and says Ecgfrid sent his army against the Scots (Northern Irish) and `miserably they afflicted and burnt God's Church' (Toulson 1987). Ecgfrid also moved against the Celtic Church in Scotland in 685 and in May of that year he was killed by the Picts at the battle of Nectansmere.

At the beginning of the 8th century, due to the reorganisation by Theodore and the success of Whitby, the Roman Church had survived the worst period in its history and was busy consolidating its power. Towards the end of the century however the pagan Vikings began their raids on the English, Welsh and Irish coasts. The prayers of the monks against the Norsemen were ineffectual and they raided Iona in 800 to 806 and Lindisfarne in 793 and 875, burning and looting these Christian communities. In 794 the Vikings attacked Northumbria and in 796 and 797 they raided Morganwg (Glamorgan) in South Wales and the Isle of Man. The monasteries of Jarrow and Wearmouth were destroyed in 800 and Norse pirates landed on the northern coast of Gaul, There they intermarried with the Franks, eventually establishing the Duchy of Normandy and becoming the Normans of later British history.

In Ireland the first Viking raids began in 798 and continued for twenty years. In 825 the Celtic monastery at Downpatrick was destroyed and in 836 the abbey of St Brigid at Kildare was razed to the ground. Thorgisl was crowned as the Viking king of Dyflinn (Dublin) in 839 and conquered

Ulster. By the early 840s permanent Viking settlements were established all over the country. The Viking occupation lasted until the early 11th century when the Irish defeated the Norse in several major battles.

At the end of the 9th century the Danes had invaded Northumbria, York, Nottingham, Cambridge and London. In 878 King Alfred the Great was forced to sue for peace and as a result the country was divided in half. The area controlled by the so-called Danelaw extended from Yorkshire to the River Thames. In 927 King Edward defeated the Danes and the English and Danish united to fight the Norwegians. In 1002 Ethelred the Unready carried out a massacre of the Danes and this led to another Viking invasion, the defeat of the House of Wessex and the rule of King Cnut or Canute from 1016 to 1035. When he died power briefly returned to the English but the Norman conquest was only thirty years in the future.

In Wales the Vikings settled in the west of the country, where they left their mark in history with such well known place names as Swansea, Caldey and Fishguard. Norse mercenaries fought for the Welsh princes and, with intermarriage, there were 'Welsh Vikings' such as Gruffyd ap Cynon who ruled Gwynedd. Eventually the Welsh and Saxons joined forces to drive out the Norse invaders. This mutual co-operation against a common enemy was to lead to the decline of the independent power of the Welsh princes and the end of Wales as an independent Celtic nation, even though it would take another three hundred years for this to happen. Although they were eventually converted, the Vikings when they arrived were pagan followers of Odin, Thor, Tyr, Frey and Freya. Their pagan beliefs obviously had a great influence in the areas ruled by the Danelaw or by Viking kings. As a result the Celtic Church in Ireland was seriously weakened, as was the remnants of the British Church in the north of England and Scotland. The pagan revival caused by the Vikings is reflected in the clerical laws against paganism and witchcraft at this period.

In the 8th century, Ecgberht, Archbishop of York decreed that anyone making offerings to devils (pagan gods), practising divination 'by heathen methods', making vows at wells, trees or stones or who gathered herbs with any invocation other then Christian prayers should be punished severely. The clergy in Northumbria at the same time were outlawing anyone who performed sacrifices, worshipped idols or 'loved witchcraft'.

In the reign of Edward (899-925), new laws were passed exiling the wicca (witch) and the wiglhaer (diviner) from the land. In 959, King Edgar prohibited well worship, necromancy, divination and rituals at trees and stones. Cnut also passed laws forbidding offerings to idols and the heathen worship of fire, water, the sun and the moon. Despite the best efforts of the Celtic and Roman Churches it would appear that only a few decades before the Battle of Hastings the pagan Old Religion was still flourishing in Saxon and Danish England.

Chapter Nine
Celtic Christianity Survives

The defeat of King Harold at Hastings by William, Duke of Normandy, in 1066 is rightly regarded as an important date in English history. It is also an equally important date in the history of the Celtic Church in Wales. In the period immediately before the Norman Conquest the Welsh Church had been forging links with their English brethren. The attacks by the Vikings on the south and west coasts of Wales had led to political alliances between the Welsh and their old enemies the Saxons. In the 10th century Bishop Cyfellicwa of Llandaff had even been consecrated by the Archbishop of Canterbury.

Within ten years of the arrival of the Normans they had fought their way into Wales. Between 1076 and 1109 they were confident enough to appoint their own candidates to the Welsh bishoprics as they became vacant. In 1107 Urban, then bishop of Llandaff, made a profession of obedience and subjection to Canterbury. Eight years later Bernard, a Norman appointee, became bishop of St David's. At the end of the 12th century, in 1188, Archbishop Baldwin made an official visit to Wales as papal legate. In North Wales attempts by the Normans to take over the Welsh Church were resisted by Prince Gruffyd ap Cynon. He reached a compromise in 1120 when David, chaplain to Henry I's son-in-law, became bishop of Bangor. Before the middle of the 12th century Norman bishops had been placed in important positions in the Welsh Church and the Celtic influence in the Church had been seriously weakened.

The rebellion by Prince Owain Gwynedd (1107-1170) in North Wales put a temporary halt to this process. In 1161 Gwynedd was determined that his Welsh nominee would become bishop of Bangor after the death of the Norman's appointee Meurig. This plan was resisted by Henry II and Thomas a' Beckett. Gwynedd was forced to send his candidate, Arthur of

Bardsey, to Ireland to be consecrated as bishop. When Gwynedd died he was excommunicated and refused burial in Bangor cathedral.

Following Gwynedd's death the Welsh Church rebelled against Canterbury. South Wales rejected the appointment of Anglo-Norman bishops and at LLandaff a Welsh candidate was installed in 1183. At St David's even the Norman bishop Bernard rebelled and demanded that, because of its ancient history, the Welsh Church should be independent from Canterbury. The Welsh monk Giraldus Cambrensis also campaigned for twenty five years from 1176 for an independent Welsh Church with an archbishopric at St David's. In 1203 the Welsh princes united to send a petition to Rome protesting at the attitude of the English bishops to the Welsh Church, This was ignored and in 1207 the Pope officially called on the Welsh to submit to Canterbury.

When Giraldus made his famous journey around Wales in the 12th century he found there were still many elements of the Welsh Church that dated back to the Celtic Christian tradition. These included the use by the Welsh clergy of the trumpets, previously rams' horns used to summon people to the pagan temples, and the wearing of the torc, the necklace of twisted metal worn as a symbol of divine authority by Celtic kings and druids . The cult of saint worship also still flourished, including the use of holy wells for healing, the veneration of stones believed to have miraculous powers and the use of 'magical' bells belonging to the saints as relics.

The end of the Welsh Church as a separate entity came with the Anglo-Welsh wars between 1276 and 1282. Prince Llewellyn ap Gruffyd was defeated by Edward I in 1282 and in that year Wales was annexed to the English crown. As a result of the campaign many of the Welsh churches and religious houses were left in ruins and following Llewellyn's defeat Edward established his own Anglo-Welsh government of occupation to run the country. Those in the clergy who co-operated were fairly treated and given land and positions of power.

The Cistercian monks, who had supported Llewellyn, took a more realistic view in defeat and accepted Edward's offer to be commissioners, tax collectors and judges in the new regime The Cistercians had arrived in Wales as early as 1131, when they founded their famous abbey at Tintern on the Wye. They were quickly followed by other Roman monastic orders such as the Benedictines and the Franciscans and this helped the Normanisation of the Welsh Church. Until the Anglo-Welsh wars the Cistercian Order had been the home of radical priests who supported an independent Welsh Church. With the events of 1282 the Welsh Church had been dealt a fateful blow from which it would never recover.

In 1190, six years after the great fire that ravaged the building and destroyed St Joseph's chapel, the monks of Glastonbury Abbey claimed to have unearthed the bones of Arthur and his queen Gwenhyfer. In one account the king's resting place was revealed to Henry II by a Welsh bard during one of the ruler's trips to Wales He ordered the monks to dig up the bodies. and they found the king and queen interred in oak coffins made of hollowed-out tree trunks, in the old Celtic manner, The grave also contained a lead cross with a Latin inscription referring to it as Arthur's last resting place. (Ashe 1957).

This discovery, at a time when the Welsh Church and people were still challenging the imposition of Anglo-Norman rule was both coincidental and opportune. To the Welsh Arthur had always been 'the once and future king'. They believed he was only sleeping, in some legends in a hollow hill, and would return one day when the British people were in need of his services. The discovery of his physical remains at Glastonbury laid this legend to rest.

The 12th century was a time of great spiritual awakening. Crusaders returning from the Holy Land had imported Middle Eastern esoteric practices into Europe. and the most famous of these crusaders were the Knight Templars They were at their most powerful in the 12th and 13th centuries before their suppression in 1308 for practising heresy, devil worship and 'unnatural sex acts ' Some aspects of what the Templars believed in and practised relates to the Grail legends and the Celtic Church. The Order was founded under the auspices of St Bernard, who was also the founder the Cistercians, and was dedicated to the Virgin Mary.

Many people regarded the Templars as guardians of the Grail (and the lost Ark of the Covenant) and they were also connected with the mysterious 'Grail ' or 'Cup of Nant Eos', allegedly carried to Wales by the Glastonbury monks in the 16th century. It has also been speculated that the sacred head or skull worshipped by the Templars as a symbol of fertility dated back to the old Celtic cult of the severed head. The full title of the Templars was ' The Order of the Knights of the Temple of Solomon in Jerusalem' and the site of the temple was the Order's headquarters during the Crusades. There is an ancient legend that during the Battle in Heaven between Michael and Lucifer an emerald in the fallen archangel's crown fell to Earth. The legend says that ever since this event humanity has been searching for this stone for its recovery will allow us to see 'the glory of God'. (Caldecott 1990). It is claimed this stone was owned by Solomon and later came into the hands of Joseph of Arimathea, who carved it into the cup used at the Last Supper. This is the same one he took to Glastonbury and which was later guarded by the Templars.

Another legend says this Luciferian stone is the same as the famous emerald tablet of Hermes Trismegistus and the emerald tablet belonging to Cham, one of the sons of Noah. In turn this links with King Melchizadek who instructed Abraham, celebrated the first eucharist and in whose priestly order Jesus is supposed to have been a high priest. Caldecott says Chartres cathedral in France derives its name from 'guardians of the stone' and the statue of Melchizadek in the cathedral holds an emerald. (1990) In some versions of the legend the Grail was the so-called Jasper Vessel, contained within a silver (moon) bowl, used by Melchizadek to administer the bread and wine to Abraham in the Biblical story. It came into the possession of Joseph because he was a hereditary Jewish priest. (Ravenscroft 1973).

The major Christian heresies of the Middle Ages - the Cathari, Albengensi and Bogomils etc - flourished during the 12th century in southern France. Also flourishing in France at the same time was the cult of 'courtly love' practised by the troubadours. These medieval successors to the Celtic bards extolled the pleasures of unrequited love for married ladies whose husbands were away fighting the Crusades. On a more esoteric level their songs and poems reflected the veneration of the archetypal feminine principle, the Domina or Lady, who was the Goddess of pre-Christian times.

The troubadours, many of whom were secret Cathars, were also associated with the cultus of the Black Madonna. This represents, without any, doubt a rising up in medieval consciousness of the ancient religion of the Great

Goddess. One of the most important shrines of the Black Madonna was Chartres cathedral, allegedly built by the Templars. Chartres was a druidic centre and the site where the 12th century cathedral stands was once a healing shrine with a sacred spring People came to it in pre-Christian times to be cured and to worship the image of the Great Mother. (Begg 1985). Caesar mentions that the druids had a sacred grove in the area and it has been suggested this was the omphalus or sacred centre of Gaul. .It is said the druids presiding over the site were visited by an Otherworldly being who told them a virgin would soon give birth to a god (Charpentier 1973).

The Black Madonna was associated with Mary Magdalene, who has we saw earlier, stayed in France when Joseph went on to Glastonbury. In esoteric tradition the Magdalene is said to have been the holder or even the receptacle of the Sangraal or 'holy blood'. Those readers familiar with the best-selling book Holy Blood & Holy Grail will know where speculation of this kind can ultimately lead and it is beyond the scope of this work to deal with this legend.

The Grail legends as we know them today date from the 12th century, but as early as the 8th century a hermit was sitting in a cave in France meditating on his doubts about the existence of the Trinity (the Arian heresy) when Jesus appeared to him in a vision. He placed a book in the hermit's hands and when he opened the volume it contained a history of the Holy Grail (Steine 1988). It is also known there was an interest in the Grail legends in the courts of Charlemagne and the Merovingian and Carolingian dynasties.

The earliest written references to Arthur are in a poem written by the Welsh bard Aneurin and Nennius Historica Britanum. These were later used as sources by Geoffrey of Monmouth for his speculative and inventive History of the Kings of Britain, originally written in Latin but translated into French for the court of Henry II and Eleanor of Aquitane, who was a supporter of the troubadour tradition. It is to the French writer Chretien de Troyes that we owe the medieval Grail romances and the so-called Matter of Britain with their tales of knightly chivalry. Chretien was associated with Eleanor's daughter, Marie, and was steeped in the tradition of courtly love promoted in her circle.

Who was the real Arthur? Certainly not the medieval king surrounded by armour-suited knights as portrayed in the Grail romances and popular fiction and movies. He was a 5th or 6th century Romano-British warlord whose Celtic warriors fought the Picts and Saxons. The story that Merlin transported Stonehenge from Ireland (West Wales?) suggests however that we are dealing here with ancient legends and myths. Several writers and historians have speculated about a pre-Christian origin for the Grail and the Arthurian mythos. They have pointed out the Grail does not fit into any form of Christian worship (Loomis 1963), that references in the legends could date back as far as the Bronze Age (Darrah 1981) and that the knights of Arthur's court were originally Celtic gods and goddesses (Cavendish 1978 and Darrah 1981). Esoterically Arthur, the Great Bear, is the solar saviour god, light bearer or 'Son of Light' who dies, yet will be reborn as 'the once and future king'. He is the sacred king and consort to the Goddess whose Grail or Cauldron he guards.

One of the most detailed, if still controversial, expositions of the Grail as a pagan symbol and Arthur as a sacred king is Jessie L. Watson's study From Ritual to Romance (1920) She claims the main features of the medieval Grail Quest - the wasteland, the Fisher King, the Grail Castle, the Bleeding Lance and the Grail itself - date back to the pre-Christian cults of the vegetation saviour gods. These include our old friend Mithras as well as Attis, Adonis, Osiris and Tammuz who all have connections with the mythical 'pagan' Christ.

Earlier we mentioned the Sangraal, Mary Magdalene and the Black Madonna.. The myth of the Sangraal was written down by the medieval writer Wolfram von Eschenbach and is connected with the Glastonbury legends. It refers to the account in the Gospel of St John of the crucifixion. John says: 'One of the soldiers with a spear pierced his side and forthwith came out blood and water' (John 19:34). Eschenbach says Joseph collected this blood in the cup used at the Last Supper - the Holy Grail. The lance used by the centurion was allegedly forged from meteoric iron by the Old Testament blacksmith Tubal Cain o and once belonged to King Solomon. It was the ceremonial spear used as a symbol of authority by the puppet King Herod Antipas and had also, allegedly, been used in the Massacre of the Innocents or first-born. It has also been claimed that the clan of Cain were in reality sacrificial priests of the Goddess. (Walker 1983)

Ravenscroft believes that the so-called Spear of Longinus was the primary symbol of the Cosmic Christ as the ancient sun god. He quotes the raising from the dead of Lazarus, Mary Magdelene's brother, as a description of a death and rebirth initiation as practised in the pagan mystery cults. He goes on to say: `The incarnation of Christ into the body and blood of the human Jesus was the descent of the sun spirit into the moon chalice, the configuration which became the symbol of the Holy Grail in the Middle Ages.' (1973).

In the 12th century version by Chretien, the Bleeding Lance is paraded through the Fisher King's Hall in front of the Grail. The suggestion is that the Lance is just as important as the Grail (Stone 1992). This lance also has the power to partly restore the Wasteland and it has been interpreted as the magical spear of the Celtic god of light, Lugh (Loomis 1963). It has also been noted that the Northern European god Odin/Woden was pierced by a spear while he hung on the cosmic world tree to gain the wisdom of the runes. In fact the Bleeding Lance or Shining Spear is the ritual weapon used to send the sacred king to the Goddess in the underworld, where he finally understands the mystery of the Grail.

In the 12th century the concept of a 'Hidden Church of the Grail', representing a more mystical version of Christianity was very popular and this idea has survived today. With the focus on the Glastonbury legends and Joseph as the first guardian of the Grail, it is not surprising that many saw Celtic Christianity and the Celtic Church as the physical representation of this hidden Grail Church.

The hundred years following the Anglo-Welsh wars and the annexation of 1282 were difficult times for the Welsh Church. The 14th century in Wales was notable for the life o the mystical and erotic poet Dafydd ap Gwilym (1325-1380). He was of noble ancestry and originally trained to be a monk before rejecting the Church. He also visited France and was familiar with the troubadour tradition. The pantheistic, almost overtly pagan, nature of Gwilym's poetry may indicate a revival of Celtic bardism and the last remnants of a heretical Celtic Christianity. It is even possible the poet was a member of a surviving bardic tradition and it has been suggested he and his lover, Morfydd, were handfasted or married in the woods by a druidic ritual (Nichols 1990).

Gwilym's poetry often seems to be in conflict with the Church's view on morality. On one famous poem addressed to a nun he invokes God and Mary (the God and Goddess?) and tells her to abandon her calling and adopt the 'green mantle'. He urges her to ' come to this spreading birch - the cuckoo's church' and forget her Christian faith. Gwilym saw the greenwood as a natural church populated by furred and feathered clergy and is poetry often contains allusions to May time and has a summery theme. Williams (1962) see these as oblique references to surviving pagan celebrations the poet has either heard of or seen. Significantly, some might say, Gwilym's body was buried under an ancient yew tree in the graveyard at Strata Florida Abbey.

In the 1380s the Peasant revolt in England had threatened the stability of both king and Church and in 1400 revolution came to Wales in the form of the popular uprising led by Owen Gyndwr. He was a wealthy landowner, lawyer, poet, patron of the arts and soldier with a long history of service to the English crown. The revolt began as a dispute over land rights but escalated into a widespread uprising when the kind ordered the arrest of the Welsh lords, including Glyndwr, for refusing to raise an army to help him stop a Scottish invasion.

Glyndwr was of royal blood and was descended from both the princes of North Wales and the royal house of South Wales. He therefore had a hereditary right to crown himself as Prince of Wales and he did so at Machynlleth in 1404. The clergy supported the uprising and Glyndwr was backed by the Cistercians and the abbots of Conway, Strata Florida and Whitland. This was because the Prince wanted an independent Welsh church but ironically when the revolt failed, and the defeated Welsh instigated a 'scorched earth' policy many churches and monasteries were burnt to the ground. The English royalists also attacked many more and it took the Church many generations to recover. With Glyndwr's defeat any hopes of an independent Welsh Church faded away.

Glyndwr's life is surrounded by mystery and folklore. Some said he dabbled in the occult arts and magic and this is alluded to by Shakespeare. There is also a strange story in Welsh folk tradition that links him with ritual sacrifice, the divine king and the druidic oak. It concerns an ancient oak that once stood on the estate of Sir Robert Vaughan at Nannau Park in Gwynedd. This oak is referred to by Sir Walter Scott in one of his poems as 'the spirit blasted tree'. Local folk tradition calls it 'The Hobgoblin's Hollow Tree' and 'The Haunted Oak'.

The story goes that one day Glyndwr, his friend Maddoc and the Lord of Nannau, called Hywel Sele, were out hunting on the Nannau Estate. Sele was related to the House of Lancaster and supported their cause. He had apparently been secretly plotting to kill Glyndwr for some time and seized the chance on this hunting trip. He pretended to shoot an arrow at a deer but instead released it at the prince. Glyndower had experienced a premonition of danger and that morning was wearing a breast-plate under his tunic. The arrow glanced off his chest and fell harmlessly to the ground. Sele drew his sword and both men fought until the Lancastrian was either knocked unconscious or killed.

Hastily the two men hid the body inside a hollow oak tree nearby and swore a pact of silence never to talk about the incident. One version says that when Glyndwr was on his deathbed he told Maddoc to reveal the location of the body after he died. In another version the oak was haunted by the restless spirit of Sele until half a century later, when his skeleton was discovered still clutching a rusty sword in its bony fingers. Th `spirit haunted tree` was apparently blown down in a gale in 1813.

After Richard III was killed at Bosworth and Henry Tudor seized the crown from a hawthorn bush, interest in the Celtic Church and Celtic Christianity briefly flourished under the Tudors. When Matthew Parker, formerly chaplain to Anne Boleyn, became the second Protestant Archbishop of Canterbury he took a close interest in the early arrival of Christianity in Britain. In his book On the Antiquity of the British Church (1572) he used the legendary story of Joseph of Arimathea to support his argument that a native British Church had been established here before Augustine. Welsh scholars were employed at the Bishop's Palace in Carmarthen, West Wales to prove this case, although there research seems to have been tinged with forgery. These scholarly monks, for instance, transformed the 6th century bard Taliesin 'into a noble clarke' of Christian origin (Humphrey 1989).

It has been claimed the old druidic tradition survived underground among surviving bardic groups in the Middle Ages (Ross 1990). Dr John Dee, the royal astrologer, seer and magus of Welsh ancestry, is said to have been connected with its survival He also has links with the healing spring at Chalice Well in Glastonbury and it is even said he found the Philosopher's Stone of alchemical lore there..

However, it was not until the end of the 17th century that the real druid revival began with John Aubrey (1629-1697), He was one of the first people to suggest a link between Stonehenge and the druids. In 1694 or 95 he allegedly revived a 12th century druidic grove at Oxford and in 1717 his successor, John Toland, convened a meeting of surviving bardic circles from Wales, Cornwall, the Isle of Man and Ireland in London to form the Universal Druid Bond. One of the later 'chosen chiefs' of the new Druid Order was William Blake of Jerusalem fame. After Toland's death he was replaced as head of the Order by the Rev William Stukeley, an Anglican clergyman and Fellow of the Royal Society, who is best remembered for his books such as Stonehenge: A Temple Restored to the British Druids (1740).

The most important and colourful personality in the neo-druidic revival was Iolo Morganwg, aka Edward Williams, (1747-1826). Iolo was a mason, poet, healer, herbalist, psychic and political radical. He claimed to have been inducted into a surviving bardic group operating in Glamorgan during his childhood At first this story was accepted until critics began to investigate further and he was accused of forging historical documents and inventing a form of neo-druidism based on monotheistic sun worship that has very little connection with the ancient religion of the Celts. Iolo's idiosyncratic 'druidism' and the beliefs of those who followed and imitated him still influence the modern, publically known neo-druidic orders.

Many Welsh clerics were associated with Iolo and his druidic revival. In 1819 he organised the first modern eisteddfod at Carmarthen assisted by the vicar of St Peter's church in the town. The plans for this eisteddfod had been laid in 1819 when a group of Anglican clergy, motivated by a desire to stop the growing influence of Methodism, decided to join Iolo in reviving Welsh culture. They were organised by an Englishman called Thomas Burgess who was the bishop of St David's and had founded St David's College at Lampeter to train young men in the priesthood . As a result of the formation of this group Iolo was able to hold the first modern eisteddfod at the Ivy Bush Inn in Carmarthen in July 1819. At this event

Bishop Burgess was formally admitted as a druid into the Gorsedd of Bards. (Miles 1992).

Iolo's own religious inclinations, apart from druidism, seem to have leaned towards a mystical non-conformist type of Christianity and Unitarianism. In 1795 he was associated with a retired midshipman called Robert Brothers who had angelic visions. He published a series of best-selling pamphlets predicting the Day of Judgement and the Second Coming. Unfortunately Brothers said this would begin with the abdication of George III in November 1795 and he was arrested for treason. Iolo tried to intercede on his behalf without success and Brothers died in a lunatic asylum in 1806. Two of Brother's disciples, John Wright and William Bryant, carried on his work and had some contact with William Blake. Bryan claimed to have been initiated by a secret society in Avignon founded by a Benedictine monk. This society was neo-Rosicrucian in nature and combined occult studies and the Egyptian Mysteries with the unorthodox worship of the Virgin Mary.

The British Israelite movement, who believed the Celts were a lost tribe of Israel, also influenced neo-druidism. One of Iolo's successors, Morien Morgan published an extraordinary work called *The Royal Winged Son of Stonehenge & Avebury* (republished as *The Mabon of the Mabinogion* in 1984 by the Research into Lost Knowledge Organisation) This drew together Iolo's version of druidism and the religion of the Old Testament. Morgan claimed to have found similarities between the Hebrew and Welsh languages and in his introduction refers to Abraham meeting the priest-king Melchizadek in a grove of oak trees. He then discusses how Moses set up a circle of standing stones on Mount Sinai and relates this to the concept of the gorsedd circle promoted, some would say invented, by Morganwg.

Later in the book, Morgan compares Jesus with the druidic concept of a supreme being Hu, Esus or Hesus. This deity is sometimes represented as a solar bull god and his worship has been found among the Gauls and as far afield as North Africa (Spence 1928). Various ithyphallic bull gods were worshipped by the Celts in Britain (Ross 1967) and it seems probable the white bull sacrificed in the sacred grove during the ritual gathering of the mistletoe by the archdruid may have represented Esus. In Gaul his cult included human sacrifice with the victims hung on trees

(Brunaux 1987) Whether Esus was actually identified with Jesus, as is claimed is another matter. Morgan says because of this identification, and presumably the alleged Hebrew origins of druidism, '..the druids glided from druidism into Christianity almost without knowing it themselves'. (1984).

Whatever the truth about the (often wild) speculations about alleged links between druidism and Judaeo-Christianity, as we have seen many clergyman were attracted by the revived druid orders. In Wales the link between the clergy and neo-druidism continued in the 19th century. The eisteddfod held at Llangollen in North Wales at the autumn equinox of 1858 was organised by Ab Ithel, the rector of Llan-ym-Mawddwy, assisted by three vicars from Yorkshire, Montgomeryshire and Flintshire. In 1867, at the eisteddfod held in Carmarthen, the then vicar of st Peter's church in the town addressed the assembly on the subject of the exclusive use of the Welsh language at the event. In 1887, William Morgan of Llansaffriadd Glen Conwy in North Wales was appointed as archdruid and invested the bishop of St David's 'with the badge of a druid of the Isle of Britain' (Miles 1992). This connection still exists today as many Welsh clerics are druids and the present archdruid is a clergyman.

The revival led by Aubrey, Toland, Morganwg and Morgan still survives in such groups as the Druid Order, the Order of Bards, Ovates & Druids and in the annual staging of the National Eisteddfod of Wales, although nowadays it is more of a cultural experience then an expression of ancient Celtic spirituality.

Chapter Ten
A New Church for a New Age?

The first attempts to revive the Celtic Church in the early 20th century seems to have centred on Dr John Arthur Goodchild and the strange story of his 'Holy Grail' at Glastonbury (Benham 1993). Unlike many of his contemporaries who were attracted to Hinduism, Buddhism and the Theosophical Society, Goodchild believed in the spiritual mysteries of the West. In 1897 he had published a book called *The Light in the West* in which he wrote about the mystical cult of the `High Queen' in pre-Christian Ireland who was a representative of the feminine aspect of Deity. Goodchild believed that whoever held the rank of High Queen had inherited a tradition dating back to the Tuatha de Danaan or People of the Goddess Danu This tradition was allegedly the ancient source of the bardic and druidic teachings of ancient Britain. He also believed this tradition had survived in the form of the Celtic Christian Church and in the cultus of St Brigid. Goodchild cites St John, Simon Magus, Pelagius and Columba as guardians of this ancient wisdom.

The year before his book was published Goodchild had a spiritual experience while staying at a hotel in Paris. A voice told him that a glass bowl he had purchased on a visit to Italy in 1885 was in fact the cup used at the Last Supper. He was told to take this bowl to St Bride's Hill at Beckary, Glastonbury and eventually it would be found and cared for by a company of women. Goodchild followed these instructions and at Glastonbury he heard a voice telling him to hide the cup in the holy well at Beckary. The plan was that it should remain there until Goodchild could find his `company of women' who would become the Grail guardians.

Goodchild was in contact with the Celtic revivalist, folklorist and seer Fiona McLeod (aka William Sharp) and before his death in 1905 Sharp visited Glastonbury on a pilgrimage to St Bride's Well at Beckary. During this visit Goodchild found a `token' left at the well by a young woman from Bristol and he took this as an omen that his quest would soon be over. In 1906 Goodchild had a vision of a sword hanging in the eastern sky and he saw this as a sign of `the Light of Christ, the Sword of Spirit, coming from the East to awaken the Cup, or Cauldron, of the Mysteries of the Celtic West'.

Shortly after this vision, Goodchild met two sisters, Janet and Christine Allen, who were visiting Glastonbury and he discovered they were friends of the `young woman from Bristol'. She was in fact called Katherine Tudor Pole and her brother was Wellesley Tudor Pole, many years later to become the owner of the Chalice Well Garden at Glastonbury. The two sisters told Goodchild that their brother had received a psychic message that they should visit Glastonbury and search the waters of St Bride's Well. They had done this and discovered a bowl made of blue glass.

Goodchild explained his side of the story and in turn the Allen sisters described how they had first visited Glastonbury in 1905. They explained that they had received a psychic communication from a former monk of the medieval Glastonbury Abbey who told them " the Kingdom of your Father is in Nature". At St Bride's Well they also claimed to have had a vision of the Holy Grail and had heard the voice of the Virgin Mary talking to them.

The sisters had replaced the bowl in the well but after Goodchild related his side of the story it was removed and taken to their family home in Bristol. There the cup was placed in a casket and set on an altar surrounded by burning candles. People came from miles around for healing and Katherine Tudor Pole and the Allen sisters officiated at communion services in which the cup was used to hold the wine. According to Benham `..they had inaugurated the Church of the New Age, a church in which woman was in the ascendant and Bride, the embodiment of the Universal Feminine, was restored and harmonised with a mystical understanding of the tenets of the Christian, (1993).
It seems that Wellesley Tudor Pole for many years had also been drawn to Glastonbury. Between 1902 and 1907 he made several `pilgrimages' to

the area, usually on St Bride's Day (February 1st). He seems to have regarded these trips as part of a quest to discover the Holy Grail. Whether he found it in the glass bowl owned by Goodchild is debatable. Expert opinion differed on whether the vessel was Roman, Phoenician, medieval Venetian or a modern copy of an earlier work. A psychometrist in London, who knew nothing about the bowl or its history, claimed it had been made in India and was surprised to see images of Jesus and Mary Magdalene when she handled it.

The cup attracted considerable attention from the orthodox clergy and eventually the story received wide publicity in the local and national press. Intelligence was also received claiming that certain documents relating to the history of the cup could be found in Constantinople (Istanbul). These writing were allegedly penned by our old friend St John. Wellesley Tudor Pole set off on the Oriental Express to locate these documents and wore a disguise, as information had also been passed to the Bristol group that agents of the Vatican were trying to reach the manuscripts first. This disguise was not a complete success, as Tudor Pole's false beard came unglued and dropped into his soup in the train's dining room! The trip ended in failure when no documents were discovered.

In 1910 Wellesley Tudor Pole met Neville Tudor Meakin, a member of an offshoot of the Hermetic Order of the Golden Dawn. Both men claimed to share an ancestry dating back to the Welsh Tudors, although Meakin went one further and told people he was descended from King Arthur. He claimed the bloodline of Arthur could be traced back to Joseph of Arimathea and the royal House of David in ancient Israel. Meakin had founded and was Grand Master of the Order of the Table Round and he invited Tudor Pole to join him in a new group called The Triad. The purpose of this group was to reactivate the three spiritual centres of the British Isles at Avalon (Glastonbury), Iona and a mysterious `Western Isle' somewhere in Ireland. This venture came to a sudden end when Meakin died in 1912.

In the same year one of the `priestesses' of the `Church of the New Age', Christine Allen, married John Duncan. He had been a close friend of William Sharp and shared his interest in the Celtic Mysteries. The two men had travelled together across the Highlands and to the Hebrides investigating folklore survivals. Duncan was psychic and he claimed to

have seen the Sidhe or Faery Folk with his own eyes Many of his
paintings depicted these Otherworldly beings and were based on his
psychic visions. When Christine Allen met Duncan he was working at
Edinburgh University and he became associate professor of art at the
University of Chicago.

Dr Goodchild died in 1914 and surprisingly, considering his unorthodox
Christian beliefs, was buried according to the rites of the Church of
England. In 1958 the land now known as the Chalice Well Garden was
purchased by Wellesley Tudor Pole from the Roman Catholic Church.
After the Great War the architect and psychic Frederick Bligh Bond, a
friend of the Tudor Poles, had designed a wrought-iron cover for the
Chalice Well which has some interesting symbolism. It features the
interlocking circle symbol of the vescica piscis representing `...the
interpenetration of the material and immaterial worlds, form or essence
with substance. The intersection between the two circles gives the piscis
(fish) or mandorla, also called the yoni, a shape representing the female
genitals which, in ancient times, was regarded as the gate of earthly
existence and spiritual knowledge.' (Howard-Gordon 1982) In other
words, an abstract image of the Goddess combining both pagan and
Christian symbolism. Dr Goodchild's `Grail' is still in the possession of
the Chalice Well Trust.

What of the influence of Celtic Christianity today, especially in those
areas of the British isles where it once flourished? Obviously most of the
sacred sites associated with the cult of the saints and the early Christian
settlements are still there in the landscape and can be visited . Those who
wish to participate in a Celtic Christian pilgrimage can even buy a recently
published guide for the seeker. This offers the modern pilgrim an inner
and outer journey around the major sites associated with the Celtic saints
and is based on the seasonal cycle of the pagan and Christian festivals.
(Toulson 1993).

Of course, some of the artefacts associated with Celtic Christianity have
either been destroyed or removed from their original locations. Some of
these can be found displayed in local and national museums. Carmarthen
museum, for instance, situated in the old Bishop's Palace just outside the
town, has a comprehensive section on early Christian monuments.
Wandering around looking at these standing stones and Celtic crosses one

at first feels uneasy that they have been uprooted from their original sites. Gradually, though the realisation dawns that if they were nor encased in the glass cabinets of a museum they would have been destroyed long ago.

At first glance interest today in the Celtic Church seems to be confined to a few university academics and historians studying the rotting bones of historical fact. However this study is not confined to the halls of academe, as we shall see, and it is actively being pursued as a living tradition by an eclectic collection of minority interest groups. They include folklorists, Earth Mysteries researchers, New Agers, modern druids, neo-pagan revivalists and even a growing number of liberal-minded clerics and Christians. This interest in Celtic spirituality, pagan and Christian, is growing steadily as more and more people become disillusioned with the modern Church and seek viable alternatives to orthodox, established religion.

The established Church today is in crisis and this is reflected in its dwindling membership. For instance, since 1980 the membership of the Church of England has dropped dramatically from 2.27 million to 1.8 million. (News of the World 12.9.93) In Victorian times 40% of the British population were active churchgoers. By the 1990s this figure had slumped to below 10% of the population (The Hidden Spirit Radio Four 22.8.93) This decline in churchgoing does not, of course, mean that people are no longer interested in spiritual matters. Recent opinion polls indicate that around 60-70% of people still believe in God or in some kind of Supreme Being controlling the universe. Belief in reincarnation, psychic powers, ghosts and life after death also receive surprising support from a large minority of people. Basically it seems that, while orthodox forms of religion are largely being rejected, interest in alternative spirituality, Eastern cults, neo-paganism and New Age philosophy is growing.

Faced with these new religious movements, as they are sometimes called, even when most of them adhere to beliefs and philosophies that are far older then Christianity, the Church has reacted by attempting to borrow their clothes This is especially true of neo-paganism, `green spirituality` and the so-called Goddess religion. As we have seen, the historical relationship between pagans and Christians has always been a difficult one. Traditionally, and not to mince words, they have been historical enemies and many of those who have adopted modern forms of neo-paganism as their religion are acutely aware of what they - mistakenly - call 'the Burning Times'. This is the period from the beginning of the 14th century to the end of the 17th century when, allegedly, nine million `witches' were executed for their beliefs. In reality the figure was probably much lower and many of those who died knew in fact were not followers of the Old Ways but innocent bystanders in a religious war.

Such exaggerations help to build an atmosphere of suspicion and distrust, with many modern pagans almost adopting a martyr complex and a victim mentality as a result. This situation is of course not helped by the genuine, and very real, harassment those interested in alternative spirituality can experience from the Church, and society as a whole, and especially from the extreme fundamentalist fringe of Christian believers.

It has been suggested that there are points of contact between the modern pagan movement and the Church. The most obvious `points of contact' are the similarities that persuaded the early converts to accept Christianity and its saviour god a another form of the existing Old Religion. However, Tony Grist, an ex-vicar, ecumenical advisor to the Pagan Federation and a regular contributor to The Guardian newspaper's religious column, wrote in The Manchester Pagan Wheel magazine in 1993 that he had been trying to build bridges between the Church and the pagan movement. He had found this a hopeless task because the Christian side either denounced neo-paganism or refused to take it seriously. Even the archdeacon of Durham, in a fairly sympathetic book written in 1992, patronised pagans by treating them as `lost sheep' who had to be returned to the fold.

Despite its liberal pretensions the false concept of Christianity as `the one true faith' is still firmly embedded in the mindframe of the modern Church. Sometimes this attitude can produce amusing moments, such as when the Catholic bishop of Brighton said in all seriousness that Christianity was 'the first green spirituality' Why? Because of the siting of rural churches in the countryside and the seasonal cycle of the Christian year. (The Hidden Spirit BBC Radio 4, 22.8.93) It seems as if even the highest in the Church have little knowledge of the pagan origin of many of its beliefs and practices.

Ecological and environmental issues are of course an example of how the Church has attempted in recent years to adopt the `green mantle' of the older religions. The initial reaction of the Church was to denounce the green movement as a cover for the revival of paganism and there have been accusations of `tree worship' and 'nature worship'. While this attitude has generally persisted there are also signs of subtle changes taking place and the development of a neo-Christian view of the environment and how it should be protected.

Some Christian thinkers today are beginning to accept that 2000 years of Judaeo-Christianity and its rejection of the natural world have caused some of the environmental problems society now faces. In the American magazine Christianity Today, Ronald J.Snider stated that the environmental crisis has provided `Tremendous evangelistic opportunities' for the Church. He urged Christians to save the planet for their grandchildren, while eliminating 'the weeds of nature spirituality before they take over the lawn' (June 1993)

This type of argument and the views it supports are representative of what we could describe as the exoteric, non-mystical tradition within the modern Church. We have seen evidence of the nature mysticism of Celtic Christianity and of the so-called `Hidden Church' in the medieval period and how this secret tradition never rejected the natural world or the feminine principle revered by the older religions as Terra Mater or Mother Earth. The pre-Christian concept of the anima mundi or `soul of the world', the Earth Spirit, survived the repression of paganism and in the Middle Ages it became associated with the Marian cultus, especially when she was represented as the Black Madonna.

Some medieval Christians regarded the anima mundi as a lesser deity or ` God's handmaiden in ruling the universe'. The concept also featured in the medieval art of the alchemists, such as Dr John Dee, who were searching for the Philosopher's Stone. On an exoteric level this stone could transform lead into gold, but on the esoteric level it represented the transformation of matter to spirit and was therefore a form of the Holy Grail. The alchemists were searching for the spiritual reality behind the natural world and `Their practice of the Great Work may have been a quasi-Christian, quasi-Gnostic form of nature mysticism..' (Roszak 1993)

The 12th century the cathedral school at Chartres personified nature as a goddess, even if this was interpreted in an orthodox way with her forced to play a subservient role to God. The monks of Chartres, such as Allian of Lille writing in 1160, portrayed her in a semi-heretical way as God's agent with the important role of creator and producer of the material world. This concept can be identified with the belief in the earth goddesses of the old pagan religions and such modern ideas as the Gaian hypothesis of Dr James Lovelock, which has a profound effect on the New Age `green spirituality' movement.

Natura, as she was called by the monks, was a microcosm of the universe. She was depicted with the signs of the Zodiac and the symbols of the seven planets set in her crown like jewels, her robe was decorated with animals, birds, fishes, herbs and trees, while her shoes were covered with wild flowers. This, supposedly, Christian image would have been instantly recognised by any pagan as their Great Mother Goddess.

The anima mundi would also have been familiar to Celtic Christians. As Canon Anthony Duncan has said: 'Celtic (Christian) spirituality is green through and throughout' (1992). He goes on to say: 'Celtic Christianity is essentially an embracing of life in its totality. Everything is sacred for there is no such thing as `secular'. Creation is good and blessed by God.' The Celtic Church's attitude to the natural world contrasted with the dualistic doctrine of the Roman Church, derived from the influence of the 4th century Manichean heresy on early Christian philosophers such as St. Augustine. This doctrine saw the natural world as an illusion and a temptation that prevented the seeker from gaining spiritual salvation. Influenced by the pagan Celtic belief in the natural world as a reflection of the spiritual realm, the Celtic Church recognised that spirit was incarnated and immanent in matter.

Celtic Christian spirituality also recognised nature as a legitimate expression of Divinity, to be accepted as God's creation and a mirror reflecting spiritual reality. Duncan sees the Celtic idea of life and religion as a unity. In his view this leads to an understanding of the total unity of existence or, as modern pagans would understand it, the concept of the creator and creation as one. Duncan believes the philosophical basis of Celtic Christianity has important links with the environmental movement. Patrick Thomas, the vicar of Brechfa in West Wales and an honourary member of the Gorsedd of Bards, also makes this point. He highlights the connection between Celtic Christianity, the pagan world view and the

148

mystical doctrine of a love for nature as the primary expression of transcendental Divinity. (1993).

The views of these two clerics contrast sharply with the less enlightened views of some of their brethren. Both writers also emphasis the important role of women in the Celtic Church, reflecting their earlier role as priestesses in the old Celtic paganism. Duncan points out that the Celtic Church did not reject the feminine and Thomas specifically refers to the considerable impact of goddesses such as Brighde had on Celtic Christianity and its reverence for the Virgin Mary. As Duncan states, Celtic Christianity, taking its lead from the old paganism, recognised the psychic and intuitive aspects of mysticism that are often associated with the feminine, such as seership and the Second Sight.

We have seen how in the Celtic Church women performed the duties of a priest and these included the celebration of the Mass. It is only in the last ten years that the Church of England has seriously debated the ordination of women into the priesthood. At the time of writing, the idea has been provisionally accepted, even though it is being fiercely resisted by the misogynistic, often homosexual, traditionalists within the Anglican community . They see the ordination of women as an atavistic step backwards to the priestesses of pagan times and believe their fears are justified by modern trends in the Church such as regarding Divinity as God the Mother or as the Father-Mother God. Many of them plan to `vote with their feet' and they threaten to split the Church by defecting to the Roman persuasion. Some observers believe the Church of England is facing its most serious crisis since the Reformation.

So far we have seen how the philosophical and theological ideas behind Celtic Christianity are influencing, if only indirectly, Christian orthodoxy. What of the practical and physical aspects of adopting Celtic Christian ideas to change the Church today? Is there any evidence that Celtic Christianity has a role to play in creating a new form of Christian religion for the 21st century?

Probably the most popular and innovative form of neo-Christianity to emerge in the last twenty years is Creation Spirituality. This movement was founded by a Dominican monk called Father Matthew Fox in the late 1970s. Creation Spirituality presents a radically different Christian perspective with the emphasis on `original blessing', rather then on original sin. Its credo draws on a distinctly `pagan' and pantheistic world view which sees God in all things and all things in God. Humanity is firmly placed with in the natural world and the cosmos, the beauty of the natural world is recognised as is the sacredness of sexuality. Female as well as male images are equally accepted as valid representations of the Divine.

Fox, who is the director of the Creation Spirituality Institute at Holy Names College in Oakland, California, has been accused by his Church of practising a `New Age pagan heresy'. On a recent visit to London he gave a talk at St James' church in Piccadilly in which he managed to mention Christ, the Green Man and the Goddess. Faculty members of his Creation Spirituality Institute include a Native American shaman called Ghosthorse and a practising witch and pagan activist called Starhawk. It was therefore not surprising that in 1993 Father Fox was expelled from the Dominican Order by the Vatican.

Some of his critics have accused Fox of attempting to revive the old Pelagian heresy, while his supporters see him as reviving the spirituality of the Celtic Church. (Duncan 1992). Creation Spirituality certainly derives some of its ideas from the mystical tradition within the medieval Church, represented by such figures as St Francis of Assisi and the 12th century St Hildegard of Bingen. She taught at a monastery founded in the 7th century by an Irish Celtic monk and located on a pre-Christian site in the Rhineland. In Hildegard's writings art and science are brought together, humanity is seen as 'the mirror of Divinity wherein the Spirit finds a dwelling place' and the Virgin Mary is 'extolled as Dame Nature, as the goddess and divine force of the maternity of all things.' (Fox 1987).

Creation Spirituality teaches its followers that the orthodox view of sin and redemption should be replaced by an alternative model of 'an integrated, sentient, still developing cosmos in which an immanent God exists' (Rev Kate Thompson, a minister in the United Reformed Church, writing in The Guardian, 3.7.89) As did many of the Christian heretics, and I believe the Celtic Christians as well, Creation Spirituality shifts the emphasis from Good Friday to Easter Sunday - from the atonement offered by Jesus suffering on the cross to the spiritual rebirth and life-affirming message of the empty tomb and the Risen Christ.

If people are not willing to be mere `pew fodder` anymore, what other signs of Celtic Christian renewal can be found in the Church? One practical example is the Order of Sanctia Sophia, founded by the Rev. Geriant ap Iorwerth of Machynnleth in mid-Wales in response to the interest of younger members of his congregation in the feminine aspect of God. Iorwerth sees the emergence of neo-Celtic Christianity and Creation Spirituality as attempts to bridge the gap between the exoteric and the esoteric, the material and the spiritual, the patriarchal and the matriarchal. (Journal of Creation Spirituality Summer 1991).

The Order of Sanctia Sophia has been founded as a lay order to develop the contemplative lifestyle so that interested people can nurture their healing and creative gifts and thereby discover the Eternal Feminine. It is dedicated to 'the holy wisdom of God' who has always been represented in the mystical Christian tradition with a female face. The Order's teaching body, the School of Mysticism and Celtic Spirituality, runs retreats and workshops offering spiritual guidance, therapy, meditation, relaxation techniques and pilgrimages.

The Rev. Iorwerth claims that at the heart of the vision behind the OSS is `...the special message of Celtic spirituality for the 90s..the Matter of Britain:.the Quest for the Holy Grail...the Return of the Goddess..the Coming of the Age of Spirit, the re-emergence of the Cosmic Christ.' He regards Celtic spirituality as part of an international renaissance of native spiritualities and cites `pagan Christian' writers like Caitlin and John Matthews and R.J.Stewart as his inspirers. (OSS leaflet, Midsummer 1991).

Today connections of a practical nature also exist between the modern druid orders and those academics and liberal clerics who are interested in reviving Celtic Christian spirituality. This has manifested in the Christian & Druid Conferences that have taken place at regular intervals since 1989. The first of these conferences led to the resolve that `a revival of the Celtic Church could be immensely helpful at this time when the Church needs to throw off its accreditions of millennia and return to the practice of a simple and pure spirituality which is in tune with nature, rather then holding a position of supremacy towards it. (Philip Carr-Gomm in his introduction to Ross 1990).

The earlier conferences were organised by Canon Tom Curtis Hayward of Stroud and took place at Prinknash Abbey in Gloucestershire. As a Roman Catholic priest in Amesbury, Wiltshire in the 1970s, Curtis Hayward had become involved with the free festivals at Stonehenge. Many of the young people attending these events were engaged in a spiritual quest, even though they had rejected orthodox religion. The canon saw Celtic Christian spirituality, with its linking of druidism with Christianity, as a possible path that would be acceptable to those who rejected the dogma, politicism and middle-class conformity represented by the established Church.

In 1989, the first conference dealt with the situation at Stonehenge and Glastonbury, while the next year saw talks and discussions on the nature of evil, Celtic spirituality and Wicca . A tree ritual was performed as well as an Anglican eucharist. In 1991 the lectures covered such topics as English bardic history, the Glastonbury Zodiac, the Welsh Gorsedd and Celtic Christianity. At the 1993 conference, held at Avebury, there were talks on Jesus the Druid, saving the Avebury stone circle and the Celtic Year. Speakers included academics, clerics, druids and an Earth Mysteries writer.

The popular interest in Celtic spirituality was further emphasised in 1993 with the publication of a new magazine called Celtic Connections. Its editor, David James, launched this publication after a small article published by the Welsh Tourist Board seeking Celtic contacts produced a flood of letters. The magazine covers a broad spectrum and publishes articles on all aspects of the Celts from prehistoric times to the Middle Ages. It also provides a contact service for people interested in Celtic culture and spirituality. The first issues of the magazine have dealt with Celtic Christian subjects such as Celtic Crosses, the Lindisfarne Gospels, St David's cathedral and the Book of Kells, but have also featured what some people may regard as non-Celtic subjects such as Megalithic sites.

Groups like the Order of Sanctus Sophia, the Christian & Druid Conference and Creation Spirituality represent the liberal and unorthodox `militant tendency' within established Christianity. Because of that their critics find it easy to dismiss them, at best, as unrepresentative, and, at worst, as an eccentric `lunatic fringe'. In contrast to these views, the evidence suggests the ground swell of liberalism and heterodoxy in the

Church may be more widespread, influential and deep rooted then its leadership cares to publicly admit.

In August 1993 The Sunday Telegraph reported that `tens of thousands' of Catholic women in the United States were abandoning their faith to become involved in `the subterranean cult of neo-pagan Wicca worship'. (8.8.93). Margot Adler, a practising witch and writer, was quoted as saying she had attended a spring equinox ritual in Philadelphia where forty masked nuns danced in front of a pagan altar decorated with flowers and goddess images. Many American orders of nuns, the same report claimed, are also actively involved in 'spirituality sessions'. These sessions discuss New Age topics like Jungian psychology and the patriarchy and 'celebrate the transcendent through female images'

Meanwhile in Britain the Quakers recently decided to accept Wicca as a legitimate spiritual path and Olivia Robertson, co-founder of the world-wide goddess organisation called the Fellowship of Isis, stated in The Lighthouse magazine (Autumn Equinox 1993) that her members included clergymen and nuns. One of the FOI members is a Benedictine monk who works for the Vatican and has helped the Fellowship gain admittance to the Parliament of World Religions. Feminists within the Anglican and reformed churches are also actively campaigning for the sexist language to be removed from prayer books. Many want new prayers to be used calling on the Father-Mother God or recognising the concept of God the Mother.

While these dramatic changes are affecting the Church, what is the response from those at the forefront of the neo-pagan revival? Generally their attitude towards Christianity, or at least the established Church, has always been ambivalent and has ranged from open hostility to sceptical tolerance. As we have seen, there are good historical reasons for the first position. Some neo-pagans are quite happy to accept Jesus as one of many other spiritual teachers like the Buddha. Others can recognise in his life the ancient myth of the sacred king and the sacrificed god, even if they have no wish to accept the spiritual exclusiveness and monopoly the Church has woven around that borrowed mythological theme,

As Robert Cochrane, the hereditary magister of a traditional witchcraft group said in 1965: ` Basically the teachings of Jesus are very near to my own perception of morality. The crucifixion is a much older story of hundreds of divine kings who died on the tau cross of the kerm oak'. He goes on to say: 'The fault with Christianity lies in the apostles and the churches, not its founder.' Referring to comparisons between the Virgin Mary and the Goddess, Cochrane concludes: 'As for the visions of the Virgin, people see God in basic images that belong to the racial consciousness, not in images that an external power has foisted upon them.'.

Whether the rapidly expanding pagan movement can come to any form of agreement or accommodation with the Church, or indeed whether it should even try, is a matter upon which strong opinions are expressed on both sides. Many followers of so-called alternative spirituality see the Church as a monolithic and totalitarian power structure more concerned with politics then spiritual concerns and the real problems facing our society. Recent factors such as the rise of extreme religious fundamentalism, the inability of the Roman Church to abandon its objections to birth control in the face of global over-population, Christianity's lack of clear direction or policy on environmental issues, the rejection of its teachings and moral leadership by many disillusioned people in the Western world and the challenge posed by alternative forms of spirituality and other religions can all be seen as indications of Churchianity's failure to adopt to the modern world and its unique problems at this historical turning-point.

As the 21st century approaches there are progressive thinkers within the Church who believe a revival of Celtic Christianity and creation-centred spirituality will halt the decline in Christian belief. They believe such a revival will provide the spiritual and philosophical foundation on which a new Church could be built. This neo-Christianity would however be very different from anything that has preceded it. Indeed, few orthodox believers would recognise it as Christianity at all. Matthew Fox's Creation Spirituality for instance, has an eclectic 'family tree' that includes heretics like Pelagius, St Hildegard, the mystic Meister Eckhart, the pagan martyr Giordano Bruno and the radical psychologist Carl Jung. It also manages to embrace non-Christian spiritual traditions like Sufism, Taoism, Native American beliefs and even Wicca. (Fox 1983). Despite this degree of tolerance sceptics on both sides point out that whatever theological gymnastics are performed, in the words of the American witch

Starhawk: `The major difference between patriarchal religions and the evolving Goddess religions..is the world view that includes regarding Divinity as immanent in the world, not outside the world.'

This observation, which lies at the heart of the debate between Christians and pagans, was highlighted for me in a conversation I had some years ago with a local priest. He was actively involved in reviving Celtic Christian spirituality and this work included leading pilgrimages every summer around the many holy wells in West Wales. We discussed the neo-pagan belief system and he was surprisingly open-minded and tolerant. However, he said he could not accept the idea of a God who was immanent in creation. In his theological model, the creator and creation had to be separate otherwise there was a danger (sic) of `nature worship'.

There will always be those who will sit on the fence between Christianity and the Old Ways, dabbling their toes in each pool and justifying their actions to both sides. Unfortunately it is a classic chicken-and-egg situation and the crux is was the founder of Christianity the historical, all too human, Jewish rabbi Jesus whose (failed) mission was to reform Judaism and free the Jewish people from Roman slavery? If he was then Judaeo-Christianity could be seen as the biggest religious con-trick ever perpetuated on the human race. If, however, the life of Jesus, as the mythical `pagan' Christ, reflects ageless wisdom and represents old spiritual wine in a new religious bottle then the esoteric aspects of Christianity, as represented by the Hidden Church of the Holy Grail, could have a wider appeal and significance.

In recent years the Church has become more willing to grasp this theological thorn and discuss the differences between the historical Jesus and the mythical Christ. Unfortunately this discussion does not take the matter to its logical conclusion as mentioned above and is often in danger of throwing the baby out with the bath water. What could be called the Anglican agnostics, publicly represented by the bishop of Durham, David Jenkins, and the radical Cambridge theologian, Dr Don Culpitt, have attempted to remove what they all the `pixy dust' from Christianity. They believe people should recognise that these myths are not accounts of real events and instead they should be seen as symbolic metaphors with a hidden meaning.

The elimination of the `pixy dust' and the `laser beam miracles' specifically refers to the the popular myths of the virgin birth and the resurrection of Jesus. In fact some radical vicars, like Anthony Freeman of Stapleton in Sussex, have suggested that even God does not exist outside the minds of believers (The Guardian 4.9.93) Things get really confused though when the bishop of Durham says that, while he cannot accept the virgin birth or the empty tomb, he still believes Jesus was God Incarnate.

One of the reasons why the new disbelievers and agnostics find it difficult to accept the Christian god is the old moral dilemma - if God is the omnipotent god of love, as they have been taught in the New Testament, then why does he allow the famine in Africa, the horrors of Belsen and Auschwitz, the destruction of Hiroshima, the atrocities in Bosnia and all the other suffering and evil endured by the human race during its history?

This question strikes at the very heart of Christian belief and cannot be easily resolved within that context. Creation Spirituality attempts to answer it with the doctrine of original blessing and the concept of a divine force evolving with the universe it created. Neo-paganism has a similar cosmological and philosophical view, with the emphasis on self-responsibility, the human origins of evil and a belief in reincarnation and the power of wyrd (fate or destiny).

It is always possible that a revived form of Celtic Christianity tailored to modern needs and problems could provide the impetus the Church requires to leave the past behind and create a new spirituality suitable for the coming Aquarian Age. The creation-centred spirituality of Matthew Fox has been described by its critics as 'reborn paganism' and perhaps we are seeing a serious attempt to reconcile the old polytheistic religions of ancient Europe with the new monotheistic religion of the Middle East that tried, but failed, to destroy them

The history of Christianity has also been the history of a, sometimes bloody, struggle between two conflicting and opposing belief systems and world views. It would be ironic, considering how the Church has always fought bitterly to eradicate paganism, if the Old Ways should return in the 21st century in yet another guise as a revival of Celtic Christianity and creation-centred spirituality.

Chronology

This chronology provides a list of the important dates and events in the span of history covered by this book. It should be noted that some of the dates relating to the early Church and the so-called Arthurian Age are still a matter of debate and controversy among historians. In this chronology, and throughout the book, the commonly accepted academic terms of BCE (Before Common Era) and Common Era (CE) have been used.

BCE

2000-1000	Final stage of Stonehenge isbeing used as a solar-lunar temple.
1000-500	Emergence of Celtic culturein Europe.
500-001	Celts arrive in Britain. Foundation of Roman Empire. Julius Caesar launches failed invasion of Britain (55).

CE

33	Crucifixion of Jesus.
35 (0r 63)	Joseph of Arimathea establishes first British church at Glastonbury.
41-64	Reign of Emperor Claudius. Early Christians in Rome.
41	St James, brother of Jesus, visits Britain?
43	Romans invade Britain

60	Paul arrives in Rome. The Roman legions destroy the druidic centre on Anglesey. Revolt of Boudicca.
61	Paul visits Britain?
64	Emperor Nero persecutes Christians in Rome
65	St Phillip's mission to the pagan Gauls.
67	Nero attempts to crush the Jewish revolt in Judea.
70	Execution of James and other Nazarene leaders by Jewish priesthood.
83	Roman legions invade Strathclyde and fight with Picts and Scots.
90	Death of Joseph of Arimathea.
137	King Lucius baptised at Chalice Well, Glastonbury.
160	Christianity established in Gaul, allegedly by British Church.
167	Lucius builds church on Glastonbury Tor.
185	Lucius invites Christian missionaries to Britain from Rome.
201	Death of Lucius
209	Martyrdom of St Alban
250	Emperor Decius issues edict against Christianity.
257	Emperor Valerian persecutes Christians.
303-306	Emperor Diocletian destroys churches and executes Christians throughout the Empire.
306	Constantine the Great becomes Emperor.

310	Edict of Milan grants religious freedom to Christians.
312	Constantine has Christian vision before a battle.
314 & 325	British bishops attend the Councils of Arles and Nicea.
315 (or 335)	Birth of St Martin of Tours.
337	Death of Constantine
354	Birth of Pelagius (aka Morgan of Bangor)
360-363	Reign of Emperor Julian
362	First European monasteryfounded.
364-375	Reign of Emperor Valentiniam.
368	Maximus Magnus arrives in Britain
370	Martin becomes bishop of Tours. Birth of Pelagius.
383	Maximus becomes Roman Emperor.
383-387	Maximus in Gaul.
388	Death of Maximus in battle. Elen becomes ruler of Wales.
390	First monastery founded inWales.
394	Pelagius begins preaching his heresy.
397	Death of St Mart
398	Roman legions withdraw from Wales.
400	King Cunneda invades North Wales.
401	Goths invade northern Italy.
408	Goths lay seige to Rome. Legions begin to leave rest of Britain.

409	Picts and Gaels invade northern England and Wales.
410	Goths sack Rome.
412	Roman legions briefly return to Britain.
418	Final withdrawal of Roman legions. Death of Pelagius.
425	Vortigern assumes control of western Britain.
428	Vortigern asks Horsa and Hengist to stay in Britain.
429	Gallic mission to Britain o combat Pelagian heresy.
432	Mission of st Patrick to Ireland
435	Second Gallic mission to fight Pelagian revival. Birth of St Brynach. Arthur becomes the king of Britain?
450	Mass arrivals of Saxons, Jutesand Angles.
452	Birth of St Brigid.
455	Saxons seize power from the Romano-British nobles.
460-470	Romano-British campaign against Saxons.
460	Birth of St Dyfrig.
464	Death of St Patrick
470-480	St Illtyd founds monastic school in South Wales.
480	Birth of Samson
485	Abbey of Kildare founded.
488	Brigid visits Glastonbury.
495	Birth of St David.
497	Birth of St Gildas.

160

517	Birth of St Columba. Death of Brigid.
521	Samson visits Brittany
525	David visits Ireland and founds Menevia (the modern St David's)
539	Death of Arthur?
545	Synod of Brefi. Death of St Illtyd.
546	Death of Dyfrig.
560	Death of Samson
563-565	Columba at Iona.
577-585	St Aidan at Menevia.
586	Death of St Govan.
589	Death of David.
597	Death of Columba. FirstGregorian mission byAugustine to England.
601	Second Gregorian mission.
602 (or 603)	Augustine meets Celtic British bishops.
604	Death of Augustine.
605	Birth of King Oswald.
616	Pagan revival. Bishop Mellitus forced to flee Britain.
617	Battle of Chester and massacre of British monks.
630	Paulinius restores St Joseph's chapel in Glastonbury.
634	Birth of St Cuthbert.

637	Irish Church bans druidism.
642	Death of King Oswald.
644	Death of Paulinius.
651	Death of St Aidan.
655	Death of Penda of Mercia.
664	Synod of Whitby.
669	Third and final missionto England from Rome.
672	Death of St Chad.
673	Birth of Bede.
704	Celtic Church in Cumbria accepts Roman rule.
705	Celtic Church in Cornwall accepts Roman rule.
708	Roman Catholic abbey built at Glastonbury.
717	Picts accept Roman usage.
731	Bede's Ecclesiastical History
735	Death of Bede.
768	Celtic Church in South Wales, Somerset and Devon accept Roman rule.
777	Celtic Church in North Wales accepts Roman rule.
780	The Book of Kells
793	Vikings sack Lindisfarne.
800-806	Raids on Iona by Vikings.
839	Viking king of Dublin.

875	Danes capture York. Lindisfarne abandoned.
878	King Alfred makes peace with the Danes.
907	Norse settle in northern France.
937	Cymru - meaning 'companions' - adopted as name for Wales.
989	Vikings attack St David's and Cardigan.
1066	The Norman Conquest.
1107	Bishop of Llandaff swears his allegiance to Canterbury.
1115	Bernard, a Norman appointee,, becomes bishop of St David's.
1131	Cistercian monks arrive in Wales.
1135-1150	Geoffrey of Monmouth writes his history of Britain and lives of Merlin.
1160-1180	French Arthurian romances written.
1161	Owain Gwynedd revolts against Norman influence on Welsh Church.
1176	Giraldus Cambrensis' begins his campaign for an independent Welsh Church. Lord Rhys of Cardigan revives the bardic esiteddfod.
1190	Grave of Arthur and Gwenhyr allegedly discovered by monks at Glastonbury.
1205	Wolfram von Eschenbach writes Parsifal.
1207	Pope demands Welsh bishops submit to Canterbury.
1250	The Black Book of Carmarthen.
1265	The Book of Aneurin
1275	The Book of Taliesin

1276-1282	Anglo-Welsh wars
1282	Wales annexed to the English crown.
1325	White Book of Rhydderch. Birth of Dafydd ap Gwilym.
1380	Death of Gwilym.
1400	Revolt by Owen Glyndwr.
1401	Gawain and the Green Knight and The Red Book of Hergest.
1404	Glyndwr crowned as Prince of Wales.
1470	L'Morte d' Arthur
1500s	Tudors revive interest in Celtic Church and Arthur. Monks from Glastonbury Abbey allegedly take Holy Grail to West Wales.
1694	John Toland revives 12th century druidic grove in Oxford
1717	Universal Druid Bond founded in London.
1747	Birth of Iolo Morganwg.
1792	Morganwg holds first gorsedd in London.
1799-1837	William Blake is Chosen Chief of the Druid Order.
1819	First modern eisteddfod in Carmarthen.
1826	Death of Iolo Morganwg.
1860	Establishment of annual National Eisteddfod of Wales.
1888	Morien Morgan becomes `Archdruid of Wales'.
1897	Dr John Goodchild hides the `Holy Grail' at Glastonbury.
1906	Goodchild, Katherine Tudor Pole and the Allen sisters form a `Celtic Church'.

1955	Foundation of the Celtic Church of Iona?
1958	Chalice Well Trust founded.
1964	Order of Bards, Druids & Ovates founded.
1975	Death of Ross Nichols, Chosen Chief of OBOD.
1984	OBOD revived by Philip Carr-Gomm.
1989	First Druid & Christian Conference.
1990	Council of British Druid Orders formed.

Contacts

The following publications and organisations can supply information on Celtic spirituality, druidism and the pagan Old Religion. Please enclose a stamped self addressed envelope with all enquiries.

THE CAULDRON Caemorgan Cottage, Caemorgan Road, Cardigan, Dyfed, West Wales, SA 43 1QU.

ORDER OF BARDS, DRUIDS & OVATES, P.O.Box 1333, Lewes, Sussex, BN7 3ZG.

ORDER OF SANCTIA SOPHIA, The Rectory, Pennal, Nr Machynlleth, Powys, Mid-Wales, SY 20 9JS.

THE TALIESIN FOUNDATION, 44 Lancaster Gate, London W2 3NA

COUNCIL OF BRITISH DRUID ORDERS 125 Magyar Crescent, Nuneaton, Warwickshire, CV11 4SJ

THE GLASTONBURY DRUID ORDER, Dove House, Brton St David, Somerset, TA 11 6DF

CELTIC CONNECTIONS Tamarisk Farm, West Bexington, Dorchester, Dorset DT 2 9DF

CREATION SPIRITUALITY Petra Griffiths, St James' Church, 199, Piccadilly, London W1V 9LF or Matthew Fox, Institute of Culture & Creation Spirituality, Holy Names College, Oakland, California, USA

HALLOWQUEST, BCM Hallowquest, London WC1N 3XX

Bíblíogɾaphy

Ailfred The Life of St Ninian (Llanerch Enterprises 1989)
Ailviell,G The Mysteries of Eleusis (Aquarian Press 1981)
Anderson, A.O. & M.O., Adamnan's Life of Columba (1961)
Ashe, G. Mythology of the British Isles (Methuen 1990)
   King Arthur's Avalon: The Story of Glastonbury (Wm Collins 1957)
Barham, P The Avalonians (Gothic Image Publications 1993)
Barley & Hansen, Christianity in Britain (Leicester University Press 1968)
Bede, the Venerable, A History of the English Church & People (Penguin 1955)
Begg, E The Cult of the Black Virgin (Arkana 1985)
Berresford-Ellis, P Celt & Saxon: The Struggle for Britain AD 410-937 (Constable 1993)
   Celtic Inheritance Muller 1985)
Brondsted, J The Vikings (Penguin Books 1980)
Browning, R The Emperor Julian (Weidenfield & Nicholson 1975)
Bowen, E.G., Saint David (University of Wales Press 1983)
   The Settlements of the Celtic Saints in Wales (Univ. of Wales 1954)
Bromwich, R.(Ed) The Arthur of the Welsh (University of Wales Press 1991)
Brunaux, J.L. The Celtic Gauls: Gods, Rites & Sanctuaries (Seaby 1987)
Bury, J.B. The Life of St Patrick (MacMillan & Co 1905)
Cavendish, R King Arthur & the Grail (Weidenfield & Nicholson 1978)
Caldecott, M. Crystal Legends (Aquarian Press 1990)
Charpentier, L The Mysteries of Chartres Cathedral (RILKO 1072)
Colgrave, B & Mynars, R. Bede's Ecclesiastical History (Clarendon Press 1969)
Cotteral,L The Great Invasion;How the Romans Conquered Britain (Evans Bros 1958)
Darrah, J The Real Camelot: Paganism & the Arthurian Romances (Thames & Hudson 1981)
Davies, D. The Ancient Celtic Church & the See of Rome (W.Lewis 1924)
Davies-Hirsch, J. A Popular History of the Church in Wales (Pitman & Sons 1912)
Deamesley, M. Augustine of Canterbury (T.Nelson & Sons 1964)
Doble, G.H. Lives of the Welsh Saints (University of Wales Press 1971)
Duncan, A. Celtic Christianity (Element 1992)
Dyfed Archaeological Trust   Archaeology in Dyfed 1976-1986
Fortune, D Avalon of the Heart (Aquarian Press 1971)
Fox, M Original Blessing (Bear & Co USA 1983)
Hildegard of Bingon's Book of Divine Works   (Bear & Co USA 1987)
Frend, W. The Rise of Christianity (Longman & Todd 1984)
Godwin,J Mystery Religions in the Ancient World (Thames & Hudson 1981)
Geoffrey of Monmouth The History of the Kings of Britain (Penguin Books 1966)
Gregory, D. Country Churchyards in Wales (Gswag Carreg 1991) Wales Before 1066

(Gswag Carreg 1991)
    Yesterday in Village Church & Churchyard (Gomer Press 1992)
Hardinge, L. The Celtic Church in Britain (SPCK 1972)
Hadrian-Alcroft,A The Circle & the Cross Vols I&II (MacMillan & Co 1927)
Hartley, C The Western Mystery Tradition (Aquarian Press 1968)
Henken,E.R. Traditions of the Welsh Saints (D.S. Brewer 1987)
Howard-Gordon,F Glastonbury: Maker of Myth (Gothic Image Publications 1982)
Hughes, K. The Church in Early Irish Society (Methuen & Co 1966)
Humphrey, E. The Taliesin Tradition (Severn Books 1989)
Hunter-Blair,P An Introduction to Anglo-Saxon England (Cambridge Press 1962)
Hutton, Dr R The Pagan Religions of the British Isles (Blackwell 1991)
Joceline The Life of St Kentigern (Llanerch Enterprises 1989)
John,C.R. The Saints of Cornwall (Dyllansow Truran 1981)
Jones, D. The Early Cymry & Their Church (W.Spurrell & Sons 1910)
Jones, G & Jones,T The Mabinogion (Dent & Sons 1949)
Jones, F. The Holy Wells of Wales (University of Wales 1954)
Laing, L & J, Anglo-Saxon England (Routledge & Kegan Paul 1979)
Leatham, Diana The Story of St David of Wales (Garraway Wales Ltd 1952)
Loomis, R.S. The Grail: From Celtic Myth to Christian Symbol (Columbia
    University Press 1963)
Lloyd, L. Archaeology of Celtic Britain (Methuan 1977)
    Archaeology of Late Celtic Britain & Ireland c.400-1200 Ad (Methuan 1975)
MacNeill,G St Patrick (Burns & Oates 1964)
Mason, A. The Mission of St Augustine (Cambridge University Press 1897)
Matthews, J. A Glastonbury Reader (Aquarian Press 1991)
Mayr-Harting, J. The Coming of Christianity to Anglo-Saxon England (Batsford 1977)
McCrickard, J.E. Brighde: Her Folklore & Mythology (Fieldfare 1987)
Merchant, C The Death of Nature: Women, Ecology & the Scientific
    Revolution (Wildwood House 1982)
Michell, J The City of Revelation (Garnstone Press 1972)
    The New View Over Atlantis (Thames & Hudson 1983)
Miles, D The Secrets of the Bards of the Isle of Britain (Gwasg Dinefwr Press 1992)
Moorman, J. History of the Church in England (A&C Black 1953)
McNeill, J. The Celtic Churches (Chicago Press USA 1974)
Morgan, M.O. The Mabin of the Mabinogion (RILKO 1984)
Morniglion, A. Paganism & Christianity (Clarendon Press 1963)
Murray, C. (Ed) The Celtic Review (GSO Publications, January 1980)
Nicholas ap,I Iolo Morganwg: Bard of Liberty (Foyles Welsh Press 1945)
Nichols,R The Book of Druidry (Aquarian Press 1990)
Piggott,S The Druids (Thames & Hudson 1968)
Pryce, J. The Ancient British Church (Longmans, Green & Co 1878)
Ravenscroft,T The Spear of Destiny (Neville Spearman 1973)
    The Cup of Destiny: The Quest for the Grail (Rider 1981)
Redknap, M. The Christian Celts (National Musuem of Wales 1981)

Rees, N. St David of Dewisland (Gomer Press 1992)

Roszak,T The Voice of the Earth: An Exploration of Ecopsychology (Bantam Press1993)

Rutherford, W The Druids & Their Heritage (Gordon & Cremonsi 1978)

Ross, Dr A Pagan Celtic Britain (Routledge & Kegan Paul 1967)

Skidmore, J. Owen Glyndwr (C.Davies 1978)

Spence, L The History & Origins of Druidism (Rider 1949)
    The Mysteries of Britain (Aquarian Press)

Spencer, R. Saints of Wales & the West Country (Llanerch Press 1991)

Starbird, M The Woman With the Alabaster Jar: Mary Magdelene & the Holy Grail (Bear & Co USA 1993)

Stewart, R.J. Robert Kirk: Walker Between Worlds (Element 1990)
    Celtic Gods, Celtic Goddesses (Blandford 1990b)

Stein, W.J. The Death of Merlin (Floris Books 1990)
    The Ninth Century & the Grail (Temple Lodge Press 1988)

Stokes, G.T. Ireland & The Celtic Church (SPCK 1928)

Stone,A A Splendid Pillar: Images of the Axis Mundi in the Grail Romances (Heart of Albion Press 1992a)
    The Bleeding Lance: Myth, Ritual & the Grail Legend (Heart of Albion Press 1992)
    Heretical Hairdos in Talking Stick VI (Spring 1992)
    Penda the Pagan in Mercian Mysteries #16 (August 1992c)

Swinton, A The Quest for Alban (Fraternity of the Friends of St Albans Abbey 1971)

Taylor, T. Life of St Samson of Dol (SPCK 1925)

Thomas, C. Early Christian Archaeology (Oxford University Press 1971)

Thomas, Rev.P. Candle in the Darkness (Gomer Press 1993)

Toulsen, S. The Celtic Alternative (Century 1987)
    The Celtic Year (Element 1993)

Victory, S. The Celtic Church in Wales (SPCK 1977)

Wade-Evans, A. Welsh Christian Origins (The Alden Press 1934)

Walker, B. The Women's Encyclopedia of Myths & Secrets (Harper & Row USA 1983)

Walker, D. A History of the Church in Wales (Church of Wales Publications 1976)

Watson, J Ritual to Romance (Cambridge University Press 1920)

Watts,D. Christians & Pagans in Roman Britain (Routledge 1991)

William of Malmesbury The Antiquities of Glastonbury (JMF Books 1992)

Williams, B. How the Gospel Came to Britain (Evangelidtic Association 1970)

Williams, G. The Welsh Church from Conquest to Reformation (University of Wales Press 1962)
    The Welsh & Their Religion (University of Wales Press 1991)

Williams, H. Christianity in Early Britain (Clarendon Press 1912)

Woodward, A. Shrines & Sacrifices (Batsford 1992)

Zimmer, H. The Celtic Church in Britain & Ireland (David Nutt 1977)

FREE DETAILED CATALOGUE

A detailed illustrated catalogue is available on request, SAE or International Postal Coupon appreciated. Titles are available direct from Capall Bann, post free in the UK (cheque or PO with order) or from good bookshops and specialist outlets. Titles currently available include:

Capall Bann is owned and run by people actively involved in many of the areas in which we publish. Our list is expanding rapidly so do contact us for details on the latest releases.

Capall Bann Publishing, Freshfields, Chieveley, Berks, RG20 8TF